The Early Childhood Music Curriculum
Guide for Parents, Teachers and Caregivers

music
play

Alison M. Reynolds
Associate Professor of Music
Ashland University
Ashland, Ohio

Wendy H. Valerio
Assistant Professor of Music
University of South Carolina
Columbia, South Carolina

Beth M. Bolton
Assistant Professor of Music
Temple University
Philadelphia, Pennsylvania

Cynthia C. Taggart
Associate Professor of Music
Michigan State University
East Lansing, Michigan

and
Edwin E. Gordon
Distinguished Professor in Residence
University of South Carolina
Columbia, South Carolina

Jump Right In
preschool series

GIA Publications, Inc.

Chicago

Acknowledgments

The authors are grateful to the following persons and organizations for their support, interest, and their belief in the importance of early childhood music education.

PUBLISHERS	Alec and Ed Harris
	GIA Publications, Inc.
EDITORS	Alison M. Reynolds
	Wendy H. Valerio
MUSIC ENGRAVER	John Valerio
ART DIRECTION/DESIGN	The Kantor Group, Inc.
	Minneapolis, Minnesota
LAYOUT	Robert M. Sacha
PHOTOGRAPHER	Keith McGraw
RECORDING ENGINEERS	Gary Bolton and Mike Smith
	Strawberry Skys Recording Studio
PRODUCERS	Wendy Valerio
	Alison Reynolds
PERFORMERS	Nichele Johnson
	Edwin Gordon
	Alison Reynolds
	Janet Smith
	Wendy Valerio
	Nancy Volk
LYRICIST	Dinah Johnson
VIDEO PRODUCTION	Early Childhood National Programming
	Department
	South Carolina Educational Television
	Jean Chase, Director

We would like to extend a special thank you to the teachers, caregivers, and children at the Children's Music Development Center (University of South Carolina), Wendy Valerio, Director. Also to Jane Reed, Patrick Snook, caregivers, and children at the Children's Music and Movement Development Program (Ashland University), Alison Reynolds, Director

ISBN: 1-57999-027-4

© Copyright 1998 by GIA Publications, Inc.,

7404 S. Mason Ave. Chicago, IL 60638

Table of Contents

Content

Foreword by Edwin E. Gordon

The importance of early childhood education, particularly in music, has been overlooked throughout history. Fortunately, today educators—as well as the community at large—recognize more and more the value of pre-kindergarten guidance and instruction. Early childhood music education has been in the forefront of this timely movement.

Perhaps the best way to describe the crucial significance of the education of youngsters is to turn to those who are engaged in relevant research, which is outlined in the "Introduction to Music Development" section of this Guide. Specifically, numerous neurologists, pediatricians, biologists, and psychologists associated with universities and research institutes have come to believe that there are critical periods associated with surges of neurological connections and synapses that take place prenatally and during early childhood.

The research seems to indicate that if a very young child has no opportunity to develop a music listening vocabulary, the cells that would have been used to establish that hearing sense will at best be directed to another sense, perhaps the visual, and the visual sense will be strengthened at the expense of the aural sense. No amount of compensatory education at a later time will be able to completely offset the handicap.

Thus, the purpose and value of *Music Play* cannot be overstated. Informal and formal guidance and instruction in music at an early age can serve the child throughout his or her adult life. The goal is not to make the child a professional musician. Should that happen, all well and good. What is perhaps even more important is that children will be prepared to feel comfortable with music, when both listening and performing, as they pursue their normal daily lives and enjoy life to the fullest. As adults, in addition to being at ease with music, they may even desire and be capable of guiding their own children in making music.

We hope, as a result of this curriculum, that children will have their childhood enriched and adults will recapture an early childhood that, in all probability, has been lost to no small extent.

PART 1

Introduction to Music Development

Numerous neurologists, pediatricians, biologists, and psychologists associated with universities and research institutes have come to believe that there are critical periods associated with surges of neurological connections and synapses that take place prenatally and during early childhood. They believe that cognition takes place in the outer shell of the brain, the cortex. The cortex consists of neurons that are interconnected by axons and dendrites, which are stimulated by syntactic activity. Nature provides the child with an overabundance of cells to make these connections, both before birth and at critical times after birth. Unless the cells are used for that purpose during these critical periods, they are lost and can never be recaptured. As a result, possible peak times for a child's learning are diminished. For example, Torsten Wiesel and David Hubel discovered in 1960 that if a blindfold is placed over the eye of a kitten at birth and the cover is not removed until several weeks later, the animal will be blind in that eye for life. What the researchers seem to be saying is that unless cells are used to make neurological connections and synapses related to each of the senses at appropriate times, the cells will direct themselves to enhancing other senses, and the sense that is neglected will be limited throughout life. Thus, if a very young child has no opportunity to develop a music-listening vocabulary, the cells that would have been used to establish that hearing sense will at best be directed to another sense, perhaps the visual, and the visual sense will be strengthened at the expense of the aural sense. No amount of compensatory education at a later time will be able to completely offset the handicap.

The home is the most important school that young children will ever know, and children's parents are the most important teachers they will ever have. Most parents are more capable of guiding and instructing their children in the development of language and arithmetic skills, however, than in the development of music skills and understanding. That is not necessarily because parents do not have high levels of music aptitude, but because most parents were not guided and instructed in acquiring and understanding music when they were children. Thus, they become unwitting, if not unwilling, participants in an unavoidable and unfortunate cycle. That is perhaps the most important reason why well-informed professional teachers need to informally guide newborn and young children in becoming comfortable with and audiating music.

Music is unique to humans and, like the other arts, is as basic as language to human development and existence. Through music children gain insight into themselves, into others, and into life itself. Most important, through music children are better able to develop and sustain their imaginations and unabashed creativity. Because a day does not pass without children hearing or participating in music one way or another, it is to their advantage to understand music. Only then will they learn to appreciate, to listen to, and to partake of music that they believe to be good, and it is through such awareness that life becomes more meaningful.

The purpose of *Jump Right In: The Early Childhood Curriculum* is to help preschool teachers and music teachers to recognize the importance of early childhood music, to discover how very young children learn to understand music, to provide opportunities for guiding very young children to learn about music, and to learn how very young children might best be taught music. The intent is not prepare children to be professional musicians or for parents and teachers to identify or foster musical geniuses. Rather, it is to explain to them how they might informally guide young children to an understanding of music the way they have already guided them to an understanding of their spoken language.

Specific musical responses should not be demanded or expected of young children. Like speech develop-

3

ment, a child's musical development is not immediate. Moreover, in our society it is common, even with exceptional musical guidance, for evidence of some children's musical development to present itself later than that of their speech development. It is important to gain as much insight into this process as possible, because just as we must not neglect a child's informal guidance in music, so we must not delay a child's transition from informal guidance to formal instruction. The result would be as detrimental to the child as to neglect informal guidance in music altogether.

Preschool children must not be taught as if they are young adults or even kindergarten children, nor should the determination of the of their musical capabilities be based on comparisons with what adults can or cannot do. Young children learn as much, and possibly more, from themselves and one another as they learn from adults. Nonetheless, if adults devote the necessary time to the musical development of young children, and if they do not underestimate the children's comprehension, these young children will become comfortable with all types of music at an early age and will develop positive attitudes toward music that will persist throughout their lives. When they become adults, they will constitute more appreciative audiences, and they may even read a music score as easily as they read a newspaper, magazine, or book. If music should become a profession rather than an avocation for a child, it should be considered only as an unexpected benefit, however.

Consider how young children learn a language. As newborns, they hear language being spoken all around them. Ideally, they are read to even before they can fully understand what is being read. They absorb what they hear. Soon they are vocalizing sounds in imitation of speech, and typically this includes sounds in language babble that may be found in a number of languages. By the age of nine months, the typical child has acquired the readiness to articulate the necessary sounds with his or her tongue to speak the language of the culture. When adults and siblings speak to children on a one-to-one basis, they offer them informal guidance in forming words. Soon young children naturally "break the code" of the language of their culture and begin to imitate real words. By using those words to communicate with others, they soon learn to create

their own phrases and sentences. Later they learn to read and write words and sentences that they have heard and spoken. The whole process of the sequential development of the four vocabularies-- listening, speaking, reading, and writing, in that order--begins at birth and continues until after children enter kindergarten or first grade. Unless such a process, which develops through both structured and unstructured informal guidance, occurs early in life, children will not have the necessary readiness to profit from formal language instruction. To be successful in school, children must enter kindergarten or first grade with at least a substantial listening and speaking vocabulary. In addition to acquiring rich listening and speaking vocabularies, it is to their advantage to be informally guided in developing rudimentary reading and writing vocabularies at home before they begin formal language instruction in school.

Unfortunately, the typical child is not given parallel experiences in music. If children who have not received structured and unstructured informal guidance in music before they enter school are given formal music instruction in kindergarten or first grade, further difficulties are often created as a result of the way music is taught in many schools. For example, in order for teachers to teach language skills in school successfully, children need to have acquired the ability and skill to engage in individual creative speaking before they enter school, yet most children have never had a chance to perform or create music individually before they begin formal music instruction, and once they do begin formal instruction, they are seldom offered or allowed the opportunity to perform or create music individually in class. Most formal instruction involves teaching children to sing by asking them to repeat the sounds the teachers or others make. Yet imagine the outcome in language learning if children were asked to speak only in groups, repeating what the teacher said. They would learn only to imitate what others around them are saying and so would not give meaning to what they said. They might not every create a sentence of their own to express their thoughts. It is no wonder then that when music is taught the way it is usually taught in school, many school children are deprived of the chance to develop an understanding of music and are simply dismissed as being "untalented" by their teachers and parents.

When children enter kindergarten or first grade, they receive instruction in language for a substantial portion of the school day. Thus, a teacher may be held accountable for each child's language development in accordance with an established curriculum. Following standard practice, records are kept and measurement procedures precede evaluation. In contrast, children typically receive instruction in music once, and in rare cases twice, a week for a period of twenty to forty-five minutes. Because there is inadequate time devoted to formal music instruction or, more correctly, to necessary compensatory informal music guidance even though the children are no longer of preschool age, and because there is no generally accepted sequential curriculum in music, the music skills that children might be expected to have acquired by the second grade are never realized due to their impoverished instruction. Entertaining children and at best offering them a perfunctory explanation of music notation seem to be the mainstays of most formal music programs in school. If the children are having fun, it is assumed by many administrators and parents that the music program is successful. It must be remembered, however, that children can experience even more pleasure and ultimate satisfaction when they are engaging in activities that promote musical understanding. Fun is temporary, but an understanding of music sustains one throughout life.

PART 2

Music Development and *Music Play*

Can very young children really learn music? Can you really teach music to an infant? How do I know if my child has music talent? When will my child be ready for piano or violin lessons? Such questions often are asked of persons who promote music development among young children. The answers to those questions lay in the understanding of what is meant by the term *music development* and the relationship of music development to music play during the first few years of life.

Music development begins at birth, if not before birth, when the human brain and body begin to respond to sound. Many researchers (Vaughn, 1996; Wilkin, 1996, Woodward, 1992) have documented the fact that, in utero, the fetus is well aware of the presence of music in her environment. Others have documented the fact that infants can detect minute differences in melodic contour and rhythmic phrases (Chang and Trehub, 1977; Trehub, Bull, and Thorpe, 1984, Krumhansl and Jusczyk, 1990). More recently, researchers have found that some forms of music instruction may increase the spatial-temporal reasoning abilities of preschool-aged children (Rauscher, Shaw, Levine, Wright, Dennis, and Newcomb, 1997). Still others have determined that though at birth a baby receives a given amount of the potential to learn music, that potential fluctuates and is influenced greatly by one's environment until approximately age 9 (Gordon, 1997).

What does all of that information mean for parents, caregivers, and teachers of very young children? It means that the first few months and years of a child's life are the most important for creating a music environment that best assists a child in maximizing her potential to participate in formal music instruction or deepen her enjoyment of music as she matures throughout life. It also means that without sensitive parents, caregivers, and teachers, children are left to their own devices to develop their music potentials, and without early guidance in music, most children will never achieve the music understanding and enjoyment that is rightfully theirs.

EACH CHILD HAS IT: MUSIC APTITUDE

Each child on this earth has the innate potential, or aptitude to learn music. "Like many other traits, music aptitude is normally distributed among children at birth," (Gordon, 1997, p. 9). That is, approximately 68 percent of children have average music potential, 16 percent have above average or high music potential, and 16 percent have below average, or low music potential. Therefore, each child is given a certain amount of music potential at birth. To date, that potential cannot be predicted through genetic study. The amount of music potential each child receives at birth, however, is directly and greatly influenced by the music exposure, experience, and encouragement she receives from birth through age 9 (Gordon, 1997).

Music aptitude, the potential one has to learn music, is developmental from birth through age 9. At age 9, that potential does not go away, it simply stabilizes (Gordon, 1997). Before age 9, a child may maintain that music potential she was born with if the adults in her environment surround her with music experiences that assist her in the development of her ability to think music through music play.

LANGUAGE DEVELOPMENT: A USEFUL ANALOGY

Yes, very young children can learn music. To parents, early childhood development specialists, and early childhood music and movement specialists, it is no surprise that with careful exposure to music and movement and with encouragement to participate in music and movement from birth, children's lives are enriched and enhanced. What may be of surprise is that children learn music best if they are exposed to it informally, much as they are exposed to their native language. In other words, music learning begins long before traditional formal music lessons should begin. Sensitive parents, caregivers, and early childhood music and movement specialists realize that music development, like language development, is a process, not a product. The process of music development must be fostered as early as possible and allowed to unfold naturally among children.

With sensitive exposure and encouragement, children may develop the ability to speak, read, and write music much like they learn to speak, read, and write language during the first few years of life (Gordon, 1997). Moreover, both language and music development processes are most naturally, wonderfully, and delightfully fostered through play. Understanding the similarities and differences between these processes can assist parents, caregivers, and early childhood music childhood in providing a model of music play and in encouraging music play among their students.

When children learn language, they first develop listening vocabularies by hearing language spoken to them and around them. Simultaneously they begin to build speaking vocabularies as they experiment by babbling with the sounds they hear and the sounds they make. This babbling often becomes a playful, joyful game of "you-make-this-noise, I-make-that-noise" between caregivers and children as both become fascinated with the language development process. Children are continually guided during the first few years of life by persons around them to shape those word sounds of babble into meaningful orders through all sorts of games that involve imitation, repetition, exploration, and improvisation.

Fascinated with the myriad of word sounds they can make and the way those word sounds feel when they make them, children continually play and experiment with new sounds and new orders of sounds as they practice and refine their speaking vocabularies. Concurrently, they are guided to associate the word sounds they speak with objects and pictures of objects, often in playful games of "What's this?" and "Where's the (dog, cat, banana, light, etc.)?" Eventually children are taught how to recognize the printed symbols that represent the objects they have labeled as they learn to read. Finally, children learn to write those symbols as expressions of thought, often playing with tools it takes to make those symbols, and the many ways those symbols can be written.

In just a few short years of language play, children are well on their way to developing language literacy. Without language play, language literacy is stunted at best. By playing with language, children are guided by others to teach themselves to think using aural, oral, and visual symbols. The many ways children learn to think using language, lay the foundation for a lifetime of successful uses of language, and all the enjoyment that may be theirs through successful communication.

SIMILAR PROCESS, DIFFERENT CONTENT

The types and processes of building vocabularies in music are much like those of language. For music development, however, the content is not necessarily that of language, and the type of thought used by persons who are thinking music may be accurately termed *audiation*. "Audiation takes place when we hear and comprehend music for which the sound is no longer or may never have been physically present" (Gordon, 1997, p. 11). When we audiate, we think music as opposed to thinking language.

When we think using language, we silently use a system of aural, oral, and/or visual symbols to give meaning to patterns of words. When we think thoughts using language, the actual sound of those thoughts is no longer present, and if those thoughts are truly original, those sounds may never have been present. We give meaning to those patterns to understand and create more thoughts so that we may communicate with others.

When we audiate music, we silently engage in a system of aural, oral, and/or visual symbols different from those found in language. Yes, music is often performed with words; however, in their most basic forms, pure music thoughts are expressive combinations of tonal patterns and rhythm patterns. We give meaning to those patterns to understand and create more music thoughts so that we may communicate our music with others. When performed, our music thoughts are expressed through our own individual music sensitivity, and they may often be accompanied by words.

MUSIC BABBLE

Just as children are not born thinking language, they are not born audiating music. How children learn to think music is largely dependent upon how those children are prepared to audiate during the first few years of life (Gordon, 1997). Similarly, how children learn to think using language is largely dependent upon how those children are prepared to use language during the first few years of life. And also similar to early language development, much of the preparation for audiation takes place in the form of play. One fundamental way children begin to participate in early music play is by babbling tonal patterns and rhythm patterns and by moving without restriction.

Gordon (1997) has identified at least two categories of music babble. One category is tonal babble, and the other is rhythm babble. When a child babbles tonally she vocally experiments with pitch and the changing of pitches. Then, as she experiments, she begins to create songs that eventually duplicate the keyality and tonality of songs she has heard performed by others. At that point, she exits tonal babble. When a child babbles rhythmically, she vocally experiments with durations and the changing of durations. As she experiments, she begins to create songs or chants that eventually duplicate the meter and tempo of songs and chants she has heard performed by others. When a child objectively duplicates meter and tempo, she is said to have exited rhythm babble. Without an exit from tonal babble and rhythm babble, lessons on the violin, piano, or any other instrument will be little more than futile attempts at decoding meaningless music notation.

Each child may exit tonal babble and rhythm babble at the same time or one before the other. There is no exact map for exiting music babble, just as there is no exact map for exiting language babble. The sooner a child exits music babble, however, the sooner she is on her way to making music sense. Parents, caregivers, and early childhood music and movement specialists may expedite a child's participation in and her exit from music babble by offering the child unstructured and structured guidance in the development of the essential listening and speaking music vocabularies by repetitively exposing the child to a wide variety of music and movement activities (Gordon, 1997). The proper time to introduce a child to piano, violin, or other types of instrumental lessons is after she has exited music babble and when she is emotionally and physically capable of performing on the instrument of her choice.

UNSTRUCTURED AND STRUCTURED MUSIC GUIDANCE

In order to build the vocabularies of music, a child must begin to learn the syntax of music as early in life as possible. As she hears tonal and/or rhythm pattern combinations first performed by others, she begins to develop a listening vocabulary as soon as those around her begin performing songs and rhythm chants for her and exposing her to all forms of live and recorded music. Ideally, at least one caregiver spends time singing songs and chanting rhythms directly to her, allowing her to hear a variety of songs and chants in a variety of tonalities and meters, repeatedly in music play. Ideally, the caregiver also moves freely as she performs the song and rhythm chants (Gordon, 1997).

When parents, caregivers, and early childhood music educators establish an initial listening environment for a child, they offer unstructured guidance. That is, they create a music environment with variety and repetition, and they wait for responses. As soon as a child begins to purposefully babble tonally and/or rhythmically, she begins to participate in the speaking vocabulary of music, and those parents, caregivers, and teachers may begin to offer structured music guidance by engaging the child in tonal pattern or rhythm pattern exploration and conversations.

Parents or caregivers need not be amateur or professional musicians to engage their children in developmentally appropriate music and movement activities. As you become familiar with the songs and chants on the *Music Play* compact disc or audio-cassette, and as you play the music and movements activities in *Music Play*, you will become very sensitive to the music babble of the children in your care. You will learn developmentally appropriate strategies for creating a rich music-listening environment as well as for offering unstructured and structured tonal and rhythm guidance.

PREPARATORY AUDIATION

Unfortunately, many young children do not receive careful, natural guidance in the playful development of their music vocabularies through audiation. As a result, children are often relegated to engaging in mere music imitation activities throughout life. Because children are left unprepared, they lack the necessary readinesses for success in formal music achievement, and they may face a lifetime of music frustration. Fortunately, new awareness of the effects of early childhood music guidance through audiation and the development of early childhood music teaching techniques are making it possible for parents and educators of young children to prepare them with them necessary readinesses for music achievement from the very start.

Gordon (1997) defines the process of learning to audiate as *preparatory audiation.* According to Gordon there are three types and seven stages of preparatory audiation. Before a child actually comprehends the basic tonal patterns and rhythm patterns of music syntax, she naturally engages in preliminary music thought processes that make it possible for her to audiate. Following is a table of the types and stages of preparatory audiation as proposed by Gordon. As soon a child is born, if not before, she enters the types and stages of preparatory audiation. Depending on the music support she receives from her environment, she may or may not find her way through the types and stages of preparatory audiation to more mature audiation. By participating in the supportive music environment available through *Music Play,* those children will receive the best possible natural guidance through the types and sequential stages of preparatory audiation. As a result, they will be prepared for a lifetime of meaningful music-making and music enjoyment.

TYPES AND STAGES OF PREPARATORY AUDIATION[1]   Summary Chart

TYPE	STAGE		
ACCULTURATION Birth to age 2-4: engages with little consciousness of the environment.	**STAGE 1**	ABSORPTION	Hears and aurally collects the sounds of music in the environment.
	STAGE 2	RANDOM RESPONSE	Moves and babbles in response to, but without relation to, the sounds of music in the environment.
	STAGE 3	PURPOSEFUL RESPONSE	Tries to relate movement and babble to the sounds of music in the environment.
IMITATION Age 2-4 to age 3-5: engages with conscious thought focused primarily on the environment.	**STAGE 4**	SHEDDING EGOCENTRICITY	Recognizes that movement and babbling do not match the sounds of music in the environment.
	STAGE 5	BREAKING THE CODE	Imitates with some precision the sounds of music in the environment, specifically tonal patterns and rhythm patterns.
ASSIMILATION Age 3-5 to age 4-6: engages with conscious thought focused primarily on self.	**STAGE 6**	INTROSPECTION	Recognizes the lack of coordination between singing and breathing and between chanting and muscular movement, including breathing.
	STAGE 7	COORDINATION	Coordinates singing and chanting with breathing and moving (p. 33).

[1] FOR A COMPLETE DESCRIPTION OF THE TYPES AND STAGES OF PREPARATORY AUDIATION, PLEASE SEE *A MUSIC LEARING THEORY FOR NEWBORN AND YOUNG CHILDREN*, EDWIN E. GORDON, GIA, 1997.

RE-ENTERING THE WORLD OF MUSIC PLAY

Pond notes the following after his extensive research at the Pillsbury Foundation:

> Deeply rooted awareness of auditory phenomena is primary, and it is the young child's innate possession from the first moment of his or her existence. Surely nothing can be more basic to emerging musicality. First a child becomes aware of sounds, then he or she experiences wonder and delight, and then an insatiable exploration begins of sonorities as wide as the environment can provide. This process has nothing to do with music as we commonly know it, but everything to do with music as it actually exists-nakedly primeval at the roots. But unless we have been privileged to share, to experience vicariously, what young children perceive, we can in no way apprehend that music. (Pond, 1992, p. 40)

To share in what young children perceive as music means to re-enter the world of music and movement play. We know that children love to play. Through play, children are actively involved in understanding the world around them. Through play, children develop a sense of self worth. Through play, children teach themselves how to think and audiate and how to work and make music with others.

To re-enter the world of music play with children, consider music and movement to be a game that may be played alone or with others. Music and movement are like a never-ending game that should be manipulated and expressed in as many non-rigid ways as possible. Above all, music and movement are a game whose contents may be as simple as sound accompanied by unrestricted, free flowing movement, yet whose intricacies may be enjoyed through endless variety and experimentation throughout life.

IMITATION, A NECESSARY READINESS FOR AUDIATION

Children must use the tool of imitation as they babble, play, and experiment with music in order to begin to master the syntax of music. "Infants and young children experience music by hearing it, by feeling it, and by experimenting with pitch and timbre in their vocal-

izations," (*Music Educators National Conference Task Force for National Standards in the Arts,* 1994, p. 10). Children also imitate the movements to music they observe performed by their caregivers (Reynolds, 1995). Without a model of music and movement to imitate, children are left to "reinvent the wheel" of music learning. Children must therefore be exposed to music and movement performed by parents, caregivers, and educators who understand how children play with music and movement, and who will themselves engage in music and movement play.

During initial music babble, young children may not imitate the tones, rhythms, and movements of the music they observe with a great deal of accuracy. With unstructured and structured music guidance by parents, caregivers, and educators, and with encouragement for experimentation and interaction, imitation may become quite accurate during the first few years of life. Imitation is necessary for children to understand music and to make it their own through audiation (Gordon, 1997).

Mere music and movement imitation, though, leave children with less-than-desirable music and movement experiences. By playing with music and movement through imitation, however, children may naturally extend imitation into music and movement creativity and improvisation. Creativity and improvisation are necessary for the full development of audiation. Through creativity and improvisation children deepen their audiation as they communicate their own music. Through creativity and improvisation, listening, speaking, reading and writing music vocabularies become personal, meaningful music achievements. It follows that parents who encourage their children to participate in formal music instruction, such as piano or violin lessons, after exiting music babble should be careful that the instructor leads their children past mere music imitation activities.

As parents, caregivers, and teachers we can provide children with a model of music creativity and improvisation through music play. From our model, we may easily encourage children to imitate, create, and then improvise as they progress through preparatory audiation into audiation. By approaching music and movement as play, you will allow yourself to re-enter the music and movement world of children. You will release yourself from the temptation to continually perform the often purely teacher-directed "circle-time song singing, pantomiming and moving to musical record music activities, and playing along with music on rhythm instruments" (Littleton, 1989, p. ix). You will be able to focus on the music and movement responses made by children, and you will lay the foundation for child-initiated music and movement activities that encourage true music understanding and endless music enjoyment.

PART 3

Guiding the Music Development of Young Children Using *Music Play* Materials

Jump Right In: The Early Childhood Music Curriculum, Music Play includes the *Guide for Parents, Teachers and Caregivers (Guide)* with the notation for 56 music selections and appropriate corresponding tonal and rhythm patterns, at least three suggested activities for each selection, information about how to use the activities to engage in music play with children from birth to age nine, and a corresponding audio-cassette or CD that includes the 56 music selections found in the *Guide*. The materials have been created to assist adults who are interested in developing the musicianship of young children in playful and musical ways.

The authors of *Jump Right In: The Early Childhood Curriculum, Music Play* have organized the plans in three ways to accommodate persons who are familiar with Edwin E. Gordon's *A Music Learning Theory for Newborn and Young Children* (1997). First, we have suggested activities appropriate for guiding children's development through the acculturation, imitation, and assimilation types of preparatory audiation. Second, we have recommended tonal or rhythm patterns and pattern activities to correspond with some of the music selections and acculturation, imitation, and assimilation activities. Third, the authors have suggested movement activities in this series to encourage expressive music play and music development among young children, and to give children an opportunity to teach themselves how to coordinate their breathing with their tonal, rhythm, and movement responses.

Those adults who are not familiar with *A Music*

Learning Theory for Newborn and Young Children, however, will discover that the authors have described activities so that it is not necessary to understand the theory in order to engage in music and movement play activities. In fact, by using *Music Play* materials, everyone will acquire a sense of some practical ways to apply *A Music Learning Theory for Newborn and Young Children* at home and in a classroom setting.

The music selections in the *Guide* are divided into two categories: 1) songs and chants without words and 2) songs and chants with words. In each section of the *Guide,* the songs are organized by the tonality—Major, Harmonic Minor, Aeolian, Dorian, Mixolydian, Phrygian, Lydian, and Locrian—regardless of the meter. The chants are organized by meter —Usual Duple, Usual Triple, Unusual Paired, Unusual Unpaired, and Multimetric. Unusual Paired meters are those in which macrobeats audiated as pairs are of unequal duration (within a pair of macrobeats, one is divided into two microbeats and the other is divided into three microbeats). Unusual Unpaired meters are those in which, again, macrobeats are of unequal durations, but they are audiated as more than a pair (Gordon, 1997, p. 122). All music selections are short and written with tonal, melodic, implied harmonic, and/or rhythm patterns that are the basis for a musically dynamic, improvisational, and playful relationship with the children, activities, other adults, and the music.

SONGS AND CHANTS WITHOUT WORDS

The purpose for including songs and chants without words is to encourage adults to create an environment in which young children and their caregivers can focus on the content of music - its tonality and meter. The authors of *Music Play* believe that, during music activities, it is crucial for adults and children to interact musically and playfully with the content of music - its tonality and/or meter - rather than only with the content of the language accompanying a song or chant.

The authors have found that young children who hear many songs, chants, and tonal and rhythm patterns without words in a variety of tonalities and meters may begin to develop a context for building a vocabulary in music, in a way similar to that in which young children hear many words, sentences, thoughts, and ideas expressed by adults around them as they build a language vocabulary. That is, young children respond to and to understand music syntax - tonal patterns, tonalities, rhythm patterns, meters, and melodic and harmonic patterns - when they are offered a rich music environment at an early age. Their experiences with absorbing as much music variety as possible is the foundation of their music development. Their listening vocabularies, and their subsequent singing and rhythm chanting vocabularies, will continue to encourage the development of their musicianship.

To stimulate young children's listening vocabularies in music, *Music Play* includes songs and chants without words that are written in a variety of tonalities and meters. In part, the stimulation of young children's aural sense in music depends on frequent opportunities to concentrate on a variety of basic music elements: tonality, meter, tempo, styles, articulations, and dynamics. That concentration is easier for young children when music is presented to them without words. In such an environment, we can be sure that young children make natural music and movement responses, ones that are not prompted by language cues.

At first, it may seem strange for you to learn music without words to sing or chant for children, since traditional music interaction between an adult and child often is suggested by the words accompanying the songs or chants. Once you become familiar with the style of teaching that is fostered by applying activities in *Music Play,* however, you will find that your interaction with young children will be focused on the music itself rather than on the text of the song or chant, and that you will not have sacrificed for yourself or any of the caregivers the cherished bonding that occur when adults share music with young children.

SONGS AND CHANTS WITH WORDS

The purpose for including songs and chants with words is to present the variety in music content (tonality and meter) in a way that, again, stimulates young children's aural skills. Songs and chants with words provide variety in an environment where songs and chants are being performed without words. Also, by performing songs and chants with words during a music class, adults may feel that they have the opportunity to respond to music and interact musically with their children in more traditional ways.

The activities suggested for each song and chant with words are written with the same intent as are activities for selections without words: to guide music development according to *A Music Learning Theory for Newborn and Young Children.* With a large listening vocabulary from their absorption of a variety of tonalities and meters of music without words, young children can more easily use language as they begin to sing or rhythmically chant music with words.

MUSIC PLAY ACTIVITIES

Each music selection is presented in a uniform way in the *Guide*. For each selection, you will find the following:

1. The title of the song or chant.
2. Music notation and words/text for that song or chant, where appropriate.

3. Music content emphasized in the selection
   a. tonality
   b. meter
   c. other musical elements

4. Movement content adults are presenting for the children to
   a. absorb,
   b. imitate and/or create, or
   c. coordinate with their breathing and music responses

5. Materials suggested for teacher to accomplish suggested activities

6. Activities suggested for each of the three types of preparatory audiation
   a. Acculturation
   b. Imitation
   c. Assimilation

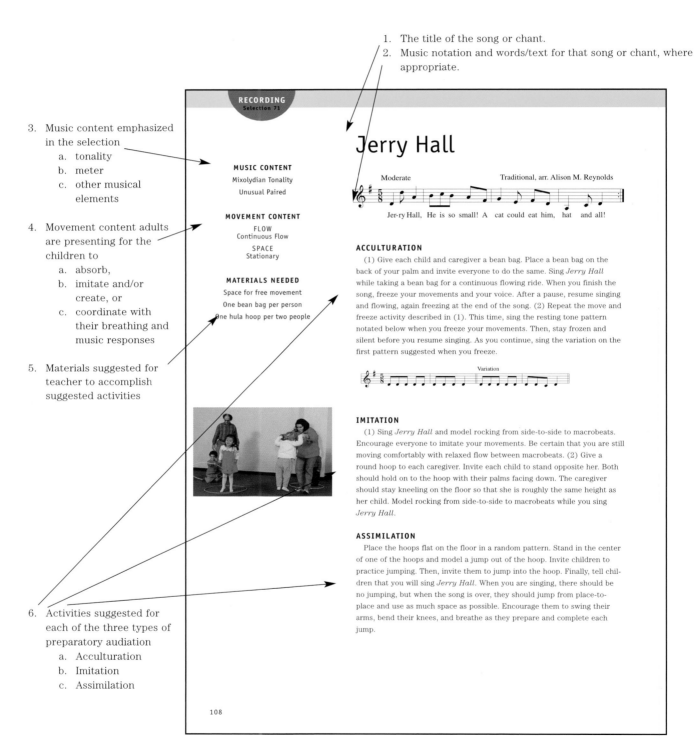

RECORDING
Selection 71

Jerry Hall

Moderate   Traditional, arr. Alison M. Reynolds

Jer-ry Hall, He is so small! A cat could eat him, hat   and all!

MUSIC CONTENT
Mixolydian Tonality
Unusual Paired

MOVEMENT CONTENT
FLOW
Continuous Flow
SPACE
Stationary

MATERIALS NEEDED
Space for free movement
One bean bag per person
One hula hoop per two people

ACCULTURATION

(1) Give each child and caregiver a bean bag. Place a bean bag on the back of your palm and invite everyone to do the same. Sing *Jerry Hall* while taking a bean bag for a continuous flowing ride. When you finish the song, freeze your movements and your voice. After a pause, resume singing and flowing, again freezing at the end of the song. (2) Repeat the move and freeze activity described in (1). This time, sing the resting tone pattern notated below when you freeze your movements. Then, stay frozen and silent before you resume singing. As you continue, sing the variation on the first pattern suggested when you freeze.

Variation

IMITATION

(1) Sing *Jerry Hall* and model rocking from side-to-side to macrobeats. Encourage everyone to imitate your movements. Be certain that you are still moving comfortably with relaxed flow between macrobeats. (2) Give a round hoop to each caregiver. Invite each child to stand opposite her. Both should hold on to the hoop with their palms facing down. The caregiver should stay kneeling on the floor so that she is roughly the same height as her child. Model rocking from side-to-side to macrobeats while you sing *Jerry Hall*.

ASSIMILATION

Place the hoops flat on the floor in a random pattern. Stand in the center of one of the hoops and model a jump out of the hoop. Invite children to practice jumping. Then, invite them to jump into the hoop. Finally, tell children that you will sing *Jerry Hall*. When you are singing, there should be no jumping, but when the song is over, they should jump from place-to-place and use as much space as possible. Encourage them to swing their arms, bend their knees, and breathe as they prepare and complete each jump.

108

DRAWING 1

14

If a song or chant has no words and is in Major or Harmonic Minor tonality, or Usual Duple or Usual Triple meter, two pages will appear with the corresponding music selection. The second page for songs without words suggests appropriate tonal patterns to accompany the activities on the preceding page. At the top of this page you will find: ACCULTURATION PATTERNS - TONAL. The second page for chants without words suggests for appropriate rhythm patterns to accompany the activities on the preceding page. At the top of this page you will find: ACCULTURATION PATTERNS - RHYTHM. Please turn to *Ring the Bells*, p. 50, *Winter Day*, p. 58, *Follow Me*, p. 78, and *Rolling*, p. 86 for examples of these plans. On the second page you will find the following:

7. Pattern Activities:
   Activities and directions to assist adults with smooth transitions between appropriate pattern guidance, and the song or chant and activities preceding them.

8. Tonal Patterns for Songs Without Words:
   Acculturation Patterns
   Imitation Patterns, and Imitation and Assimilation Patterns

   Rhythm Patterns for Chants Without Words:
   Acculturation Patterns
   Imitation and Assimilation

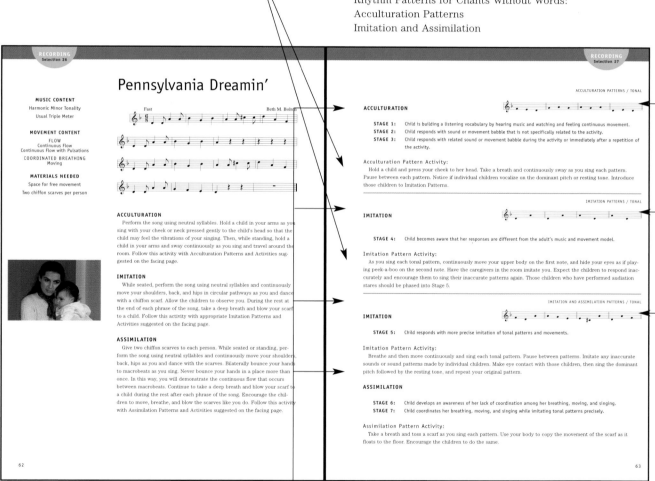

DRAWING 2

9. A brief description of the characteristics of each stage of preparatory audiation

To feel most confident while guiding the music development of young children in a group situation, the authors recommend you accomplish three basic, yet comprehensive, related music-specific goals:

1) develop a repertoire of movements,

2) develop a repertoire of songs and chants, and

3) develop a repertoire of tonal and rhythm patterns.

By referring to, practicing, and implementing activities in this book, you will accomplish these objectives. The importance of these skills are explained in detail in the parts that follow.

PART 4

Developing a Repertoire of Movements

Many researchers and teachers who are interested in the music development of young children have recognized that movement is a natural, and even spontaneous, response to music that begins at a very young age (Gordon, 1997; Hicks, 1993; Metz 1989; Moog, 1976; Morehead and Pond, 1978; Reynolds, 1995; Sims, 1985). During the second half of the 20th century, there have been numerous studies to determine how movement can be used best in an early childhood music environment, and how it provides the most long-term benefits for children. Several researchers (Gordon, 1997; Hicks, 1993; Moog, 1976; Reynolds, 1995) have found movement to be very important in conjunction with the music development of young children.

Moog (1976) was the first researcher to study young children who were performing natural music and movement responses. He observes that, when young children babble in music, they tend to move their whole bodies in ways that are coordinated with their babble. He suggests that is the case because, when a child breathes, the breathing mechanisms are coordinated naturally. Therefore, her coordinated vocalizations and any other coordinated body movements she performs are natural outgrowths of her coordinated breathing.

The implications of Moog's study are in direct opposition to most of the traditional, regularly-scheduled music and movement experiences designed for young children. Traditionally, adults are anxious for very young children to respond to music in their environment in coordinated ways to the music that the adults are making, by moving to and chanting to steady beats in steady tempos, and by engaging in singing whole songs in tune. Instead, the observations that Moog recorded imply that adults should be sensitive to the varying degrees to which young children are able to coordinate themselves with their own music babble. Children should be gradually guided to coordinate their breathing and moving with music an adult is performing or asking the children to perform. To emerge from one's music babble is to understand the syntax of music performed by others in one's culture. It is possible that

movement is the most important vehicle for assisting a young child in making the transition from music babble to music sense.

Gordon (1997), supporting Moog's interpretation in *A Music Learning Theory for Newborn and Young Children,* believes that movement may be the key to a young child's music development, in that it assists her with developing her own coordination. Her coordination should develop as she becomes acculturated to and imitates the music syntax of adults, gradually becoming aware on her own that she lacks coordination between her breathing and her moving and singing or moving and chanting when listening to the adults' music. Then, of equal importance, Gordon believes that movement assists the child with realizing that she needs to begin to teach herself how to maintain the coordination between her breathing and moving and singing or moving and chanting while performing music - that is, actually singing or chanting. Gordon specifies the type of movements that best guide children from babble into syntax.

The movements Gordon suggests are based upon the interaction of movement elements that Rudolf von Laban analyzed and labeled as he observed dancers: Time, Weight, Space, and Flow (1971). Laban believed that every time we move we exert effort in an interacting combination of those elements. Each element, in isolation, exists along a continuum for which the quality of a movement at each extremity is described. Time exists as sustained (slow) or quick durations; weight as strong or gentle sensations of body weight; space as direct or indirect in focus; and flow as free or bound bodily tension. Laban advocated that dancers have positive control of their bodies as they perform movements that emphasizes time, weight, space, and flow in isolation before they combine these elements in rhythmic movement or specific dance steps within dance styles.

In essence, Laban was saying that a dancer should learn to coordinate her body independent of learning specific dance steps, rather than through repeated drill and practice of specific steps or combinations. In a similar way, researchers are discovering that very young children can teach themselves to coordinate their bodies at the same time they are exiting tonal and rhythm babble in their early years rather than trying to be taught coordination and music syntax during formal instruction in general music and instrumental music in their later years (Gordon, 1997; Reynolds, 1995).

By adapting Laban's effort elements to assist young children in teaching themselves to become coordinated for musical purposes rather than dance purposes, it is useful to present the elements in this order: Flow, emphasizing continuous free-flowing movement; Weight, emphasizing strong and gentle movement; Space, emphasizing self-space and shared space, stationary and locomotor movements, making and filling up spaces, and moving in different directions, and at different levels, using straight and curvy pathways; and Time, emphasizing first quick and slow, flow and eventually incorporating the coordination of movement to the music.

It seems that a young child who is exiting tonal and rhythm babble and a mature musician share a fundamental task: to be fully aware of ones' whole body. We are observing that young children are able to teach themselves such awareness by engaging their whole bodies in flowing movement that is continuous, uses curvy pathways in lots of space, and emphasizes a variety of body parts—especially hips, backs, and shoulders. Because energy and tension are ever-present in each of our bodies, moving with continuous flow allows us to positively control our energy and tension. If we are able to positively control energy and tension, first through actual physical movement and, later, through internalizing that movement, we will less likely displace our energy as we engage in music performance. That is, we will breathe, draw the bow, reach for an upper octave, finger a difficult passage, and accurately begin to play again after long pauses in the music, all while

not rushing or slowing the tempo of the music. Moreover, for the young child first to observe musicians who are relaxed and able to move with continuous flow, and then to imitate that movement and successfully engage in continuous flow herself is essential to guide the child to coordinate her breathing and singing and/or chanting.

The use of Laban's effort elements also has been adapted by conductors, whose gestures must communicate expression, style, articulation, shapes of phrases, dynamics, tempo, meter, precision, and breathing (Jordan, 1996). For the conductor, musical expression is condensed into gestures with variations in emphases on flow, weight, space, and time. The early childhood music educator must be aware of and consider her whole body to be a model of musical expression for young children as they are engaging in music play. When young children observe an adult who is using continuous flow to communicate with sensitivity the style and expressiveness of a song or chant, they naturally absorb and begin to imitate both, eventually incorporating a sense of style and expressiveness into their musical performances. For all musicians, it seems that the difference between an accurate performance and a musical performance is dependent upon the effective incorporation of flow, weight, space, and time.

Researchers (Hicks, 1993; Reynolds, 1995) have shown that children as young as 10 months to three years of age are able to imitate continuous flowing movements with individual body parts as well as with their whole bodies. Moreover, children who perform tonal and rhythm vocal responses with expression are those who have demonstrated use of continuous flow (Reynolds, 1995).

The authors of this curriculum have found that movement activities that emphasize the movement elements identified and labeled by Laban - Time, Weight, Space, and Flow - are useful when adapted to coincide with Gordon's interpretations of how to develop musicianship. Understanding why these types of movements are essential, as well as how to demonstrate them as you guide the music development of young children, will assist you as you interpret the descriptions within activities in *Music Play* in conjunction with songs, tonal patterns, chants, rhythm patterns, and the types and stages of preparatory audiation.

WHAT TYPES OF MOVEMENTS DO I NEED TO FEEL COMFORTABLE MODELING?

For each of the activities that accompany the 56 music selections, there are suggested movements that assist young children in various types and stages of preparatory audiation. Those are listed under *Movement Content* at the beginning of each plan. A description of those types of movements follows. With the exception of inviting childen to move with continuous flow with pulsations, all movements in *Music Play* are useful for guiding children through all types and stages of preparatory audiation. The use of continuous flow with pulsations should be reserved for activities with children who are in stages 6 and 7 of preparatory audiation.

FLOW

For many of the activities in *Music Play,* you will find "continuous flow" listed under *Movement Content.* For reasons already described, this is the most important type of movement that you can develop for yourself. The authors hope that it becomes natural for you to model continuous flow as you engage in activities for music and movement play. In order to be able to move with continuous flow, think also of swimming movements using your whole body that can be described as relaxed, free, flexible, fluid, uninterrupted, circular, and smooth to assist you.

Begin by increasing the extent to which you are aware of different parts of your body and how each can be moved with flow. Try an idea we learned from Jane Kahan. As you stand in silence, move only one body part, such as your hand or arm, with continuous flow. To move with continuous flow, imagine that you are holding an object in your hand and that you want to take that object for a ride - a smooth, continuous ride in curvy pathways that moves all around and behind

you in the space where you stand. (Don't be concerned about "holding" the object - it won't fall off of your hand!) Shift the imaginary object to your elbow. Your whole arm will continue to move, but you will be emphasizing a different body part as you lead the ride with your elbow. Even though your whole arm will continue to move, leading continuous flow with your elbow probably will feel different, and it most likely will look different too. Someone else who is watching you would be able to tell whether you were emphasizing your hand or your elbow with your continuous flow. Move your hand, arm, or elbow in circular pathways through the air rather than straight lines, and you will achieve more continuity in your flowing movement.

If you continue such rides with other body parts, such as your head, nose, shoulders, back, hips, knees, toes, and legs, you will continue to increase your body awareness and experience how different parts can move with flow. When you are comfortable, move in front of a full-length mirror to observe how continuous flow looks rather than relying entirely upon how continuous flow feels. As a future movement model, you want to be certain that caregivers and children in the music environment are able to look to you to see what to do in the same way they will listen to you to hear what to do! Try to take more adventurous rides that use a lot of space as you stay in one place and move various body parts.

Return to continuous flowing movement, this time emphasizing your hips. Be certain that you are moving your hips in a circular pathway and that you remember to bend your knees while doing so. If you accomplish both the circular movement led by your hips as well as remembering to bend your knees, you most likely will find that 100% of your body is engaged in movement. The hips are your key to engaging your whole body in flow.

WEIGHT

After you are certain that your continuous flow movement model incorporates your hips, shoulders, and back and a variety of other body parts in a relaxed way, you are ready to add the second element to your movement model: Weight. The sensation of continuous flow in which you are varying the force behind it perhaps is most easily understood by continuing with the "giving rides" activity. If you place imaginary light-weight, or gentle and precious objects on your hips, hands, shoulders, back, and knees and begin to give those objects smooth rides, you most likely will experience gentle continuous flow. Although you may be tempted only to move slowly with your precious objects, you will find the element Time- how quickly or slowly you move - not to be crucial for gentle continuous flow. (As an experiment, move the precious objects on various body parts with gentle continuous flow as quickly, and then as slowly, as you can. Then, realize that Time will be addressed in isolation after Weight and Space.)

In contrast to gentle continuous flow, replace the imaginary objects on your body with heavy objects. Although you may be tempted to stoop down from the sheer "weight" of your new load, decide to stand tall and move with continuous flow as you did in the initial "giving rides" activity described previously. Respond to the weight difference of the load you are carrying. Now intersperse random changes from gentle, precious, or light objects to heavy, strong objects - all the while not changing how quickly or slowly you are moving. Does it feel different to move gently than to move with strong continuous flow? Does strong movement look different from gentle movement? Even the subtle differences along the continuum of gentle and strong in your continuous flowing movement model will be absorbed and imitated by very young children.

SPACE

All of the continuous flow movements thus far have included, but not emphasized, some parts of the third element of Laban's movement labels: Space. There are several ways in which the authors have asked you to model Space while performing movements during activities found in *Music Play*. First and foremost, using large amounts of Space as you engage in continuous flow will insure that young children and adults in the music environment will pay attention to, absorb, and imitate your continuous flow.

In *Music Play*, the use of the term *self space* means that each person is moving without touching anybody or anything, and *shared space* means that it is possible to move while touching another person or another thing, such as an instrument or a prop, during an activity. Self-and shared-space movement can occur in one place, referred to as *stationary space,* or it can occur

as people are traveling from one place to another about the room, referred to as *locomotor space.* You can be in space at varying *levels,* standing and reaching at high, bending at medium, or stooping or lying at low levels.

To continue, it is possible to take up a lot of space or hardly any space as you are moving in stationary, locomotor, self, shared, high, medium, or low space by making open shapes or closed shapes. *Open shapes* are made with no limbs and appendages touching, and *closed shapes* are made when limbs and appendages are touching. Those open or closed shapes can be formed using angular, *straight shapes,* or by using rounded, *curvy shapes.* Finally, movements can be performed moving forward, backward, diagonally, or sideways in relation to an object or person while facing forward, backward, or sideways and while moving along *straight pathways* or *curvy pathways* in the air or on the floor while using locomotor movement to vary the use of space. Remember, it is the use of circular or curvy pathways in the air that assists you in moving with continuous flow.

TIME

The last of Laban's four elements is Time. Laban used the words sustained and quick. We have modified those words to slow and quick. Time is perhaps the easiest to understand and to model, especially in conjunction with continuous flow. As in your previous experiment, give a continuous flowing ride with neutral attention to Weight, and then make variations in the speed of your ride. Move individual body parts with quick flow, then slow flow. Gradually add more body parts so that you are able to move your whole body quickly or slowly. Remember to move your hips!

PULSATING MOVEMENTS

Another movement you often will find listed under *Movement Content* is "continuous flow with pulsations." This type of movement is useful for assisting children who are phasing through stages 6 and 7 of preparatory audiation. Now that you are able to move with continuous flow in conjunction with varying degrees of Weight, different categories of Space, and/or variations of Time, experiment with continuous flow with pulsations. Once again, "giving rides" is useful for this experience.

Instead of giving smooth rides, try to give bumpy rides. You may find this easiest if you return to giving only your hand a ride. Can you put bumps into your hand's ride? (Because you are moving in silence, you will not need to worry about coordinating your bumps to a pulse in the music.) The most difficult aspect of this type of movement is to continue using Flow and Space as your hand travels over the bumps. Put each "bump" in a different place in space in space to assist your Flow.

After you have used your hand, use isolated body parts as you did when beginning to move with continuous flow. Which body part is most important for moving the whole body with continuous flow with pulsations? You guessed it! If you can take your hips for a bumpy, curvy ride successfully, it is likely your whole body will be engaged in continuous flow with pulsations. Eventually, as your whole body moves with pulsations, your shoulders, back, elbows, and even your head will be modeling those pulsations. The pulsations are not jolts, but rather gentle dabs in space. As recommended previously, take your movements to a full-length mirror to determine whether you are satisfied with how your model will look to the children and other adults in your music classes.

The purpose of moving with continuous flow and pulsations is to be able to model those pulsations in coordination with microbeats in songs, rhythm chants, and rhythm patterns that you are performing. Young children typically attend to microbeats before macrobeats when responding with rhythmic movements or chanting. The final step in preparing continuous flow with pulsations is to be certain you are able to maintain this movement while actually performing rhythm patterns, or rhythm chants, or while chanting BAH to macrobeats in Usual Duple meter at various tempos. If you are having some difficulty doing those three tasks, ask yourself whether it is because you are not audiating the song, chant, rhythm patterns, or macrobeats successfully. If you decide that none of these are the problem, it may be useful for you to practice coordinating your continuous flow with pulsations to the *Music Play* recordings of songs, chants, and rhythm patterns in Usual Duple meter before trying to sing or chant and move simultaneously.

PART 5

Developing a Repertoire of Songs and Chants

Songs and chants, combined with movement, are the fundamentals of your music class, and the success of your music guidance relies on the degree to which you have established a suitable repertoire of each. First, select music from the series that you enjoy hearing. Be certain to analyze selections for music content - tonality and meter - so that your repertoire of songs and chants represents variety rather than sameness of tonality or meter. If you have a repertoire of at least 20 selections (4 of which also suggest tonal patterns and 4 of which also suggest rhythm patterns) for a 10-week *Music Play* session, then you will be poised to be successful in interacting with young children in music.

In order to develop a repertoire, we are not suggesting that you select 20 songs and chants and *memorize* them for performing in front of a group. Instead, we are suggesting that you learn each selection through *audiation,* which means that you comprehend the varied content of that music. In this way, you are not only able to sing the whole melody or chant the whole chant, but you are able to play with the music by hearing and performing the various parts of it, such as hearing and singing the resting tone (theoretically referred to as the tonic) at any given point of a song, and feeling and moving to the macrobeats (the larger pulse) and the microbeats (the smaller pulses) that correspond to the music. Taking this one step further, being able to audiate the harmonies implied underneath the melodies or to audiate suitable variations in the types of rhythm patterns used predominantly in a chant or melodic rhythm allows you to play with or *improvise* with those aspects of the music as you guide young children. Usually, when you understand a piece of music in these ways, you will find that you don't "forget how the music goes" because you understand what the music IS.

After you have accumulated a few songs and chants for your repertoire, practice singing them around the house, as you drive to work, or as you wait for a bus! Can you think through (audiate) an entire song or chant in "real time" in your head? Sing a song in "real time" in your head again, but keep stopping to sing the resting tone out loud! Chant a chant in "real time" in your head again, but this time, move to macrobeats and microbeats as you do so. How did you do? You have begun to understand audiation!

In the *Guide,* find an activity suggested with a song or a chant you have learned. Perform any of the suggested movement activities to discover that you can move and sing or chant at the same time. What other parts of the activities can you implement on your own? Can you improvise a different ending to the song or chant? Can you create another section to the existing music that is different from, but incorporates musical ideas from the original song or chant? Can you create tonal patterns and/or rhythm patterns that correspond with the original tonality and/or meter of the song or chant without looking at music notation? (Please refer to the next section to learn more about tonal and rhythm patterns.) If so, you are audiating and have begun to understand *Music Play!*

PART 6

Developing a Repertoire of Tonal and Rhythm Patterns

Once you are able to sing songs without words in Major or Harmonic Minor tonality or chant chants without words in Usual Duple or Usual Triple meter, then develop a tonal pattern and a rhythm pattern vocabulary to sing and chant. In *Music Play,* tonal patterns refer to two-, three-, or occasionally four-note patterns that contain different pitches without variations in rhythm durations. Rhythm patterns contain variations in rhythm durations that clearly establish a meter, and are performed with inflection but without different pitches. As with learning a repertoire of songs and chants, the authors do not advocate that you *memorize* the patterns suggested in this part of the *Guide,* heard on the *Music Play* recording, or notated on the second pages of plans accompanying appropriate selections in the *Guide.* Instead, become familiar with the principles of pattern guidance, the patterns that are appropriate for different types of preparatory audiation, and then develop your pattern vocabulary through *audiation* in much the same way you did while developing your song and chant repertoires.

Pattern guidance is included during the 30-minute class for three reasons:

1. Pattern guidance provides an opportunity for you and each young child to interact one-on-one with a smaller part of the musical whole (the whole song or whole chant). That is, tonal patterns assist children in hearing the syntax of a tonality and rhythm patterns assist children in hearing the syntax of a meter.

2. Pattern guidance, in part, assists you with monitoring and insuring the progress of each young child's music development. As you become familiar with the types of tonal and rhythm responses young children typically perform during a series of music classes, you will be able to make decisions about the tonal and rhythm patterns and the types of activities that each

young child requires to progress successfully through the types and stages of preparatory audiation. A young child's music-listening vocabulary will be the basis for her building a thoughtful singing and chanting vocabulary through a process similar to that for language acquisition described earlier: she absorbs, listens to, first responds inaccurately, then imitates more precisely, and eventually, coordinates her breathing and moving with her tonal and rhythm pattern responses. Later, children can be given the opportunity to combine and apply their pattern vocabularies when singing whole songs or chanting whole chants.

3. Pattern guidance for young children exists primarily to expose tonal and rhythm patterns to young children so they can begin to hear *how* to audiate music they are absorbing. Later, during formal instruction in public school, children will build on that foundation as they learn *what* to audiate when listening to music.

TONAL PATTERN GUIDANCE

Usually, tonal patterns and pattern activities are presented directly following a song that has been sung in the same tonality and the same keyality. The preceding song places the content of the patterns in a musical context by establishing the syntax of the tonality for children. As described previously, all tonal patterns are sung for children without rhythm and meter. Please refer to *Ring the Bells,* page 50, or pages 24, 27, and 28 of this section for examples of tonal patterns. In general, it is important to realize that "the opportunity for young children to hear the patterns' syntax during preparatory audiation is more important than their correct performance of tonal patterns" (Gordon, 1997).

Tonal pattern guidance requires the teacher to learn three basic sets of tonal patterns.

1. Acculturation Patterns: Stages 1 - 3 of preparatory audiation,

2. Imitation Patterns: Stage 4 of preparatory audiation, and

3. Imitation and Assimilation Patterns: Stage 5, and Stages 6 and 7 of preparatory audiation, respectively.

A complete description of the types and stages of preparatory audiation and tonal pattern guidance can be found in *A Music Learning Theory for Newborn and Young Children* (Gordon, 1997).

There are elements common to tonal pattern guidance, regardless of the type of tonal patterns you are presenting. The tonal patterns should be, as mentioned previously, in the same tonality and the same keyality as the song immediately preceding them. If you are singing selections as notated and recorded in *Music Play,* those selections feature the singing range of young children, which is approximately from D above middle C to A, a perfect fifth above (Gordon, 1997).

To perform a tonal pattern, take a full, deep breath and sing. The patterns should be performed with a pleasant singing voice quality that does not incorporate excessive vibrato. Use a neutral syllable to perform the patterns, such as "bum" or even sounds that babbling infants and toddlers make spontaneously, such as "mah," "yah," or "yeh." Make eye contact with the child to whom you are singing and smile, just as you would if you were speaking or listening to her.

After you sing a tonal pattern to a young child, your pattern may be followed by silence–a listening response. It is important that you ask the other adults sometimes to be silent following your patterns. It is often during the silences that a child to whom you are singing, or even another child across the room, will vocalize or sing responses. After singing two or three patterns to a young child for her to absorb, you may invite another adult to be your echo. Sing a tonal pattern. After a brief pause, give a "breathe and sing" gesture to assist the adult with being your echo. The brief pauses between each tonal pattern and the "breathe and sing" gesture should be of varying lengths so that tonal pattern guidance does not begin to include a steady beat. Be certain that the adult also models, or the group of caregivers also model, a full, deep breath before singing, and that adults also sing wth a pleasant singing quality without excessive vibrato. During *all stages* of tonal guidance, it is appropriate for you and the caregivers to model continuous flow.

TONAL PATTERN GUIDANCE
ACCULTURATION PATTERNS: STAGES 1 - 3

Adults should neither expect nor physically or verbally encourage young children to respond to tonal pattern guidance in the Acculturation type of preparatory audiation. This is especially important and sometimes difficult to communicate to caregivers. To become acculturated in music, fundamentally, is to absorb the syntax - in this case, the tonality - of the music being presented. Absorption, not performance, is the purpose of using tonal patterns at this point in a young child's music development.

Acculturation Patterns are step-wise, diatonic, patterns with three pitches. The three pitches should be sung *legato,* each pitch lasting the same duration, with the first consonant of the chosen neutral syllable repeated for each pitch, such as "bum, bum, bum" or "yah, yah, yah." *Legato* singing is closely related to the type of vocal response that very young children babble easily and frequently, whether stimulated by language, music, facial expressions, or all three. *During all three stages of the Acculturation type of preparatory audiation, it is appropriate to model continuous flow using any and all parts of your body.* Ask caregivers to copy your movements. Do not, however, expect or ask young children to do the same.

If silence usually follows your tonal Acculturation Pattern, a child eventually will babble different types of vocal responses while she is in the Acculturation type of preparatory audiation. If the child is in Stage 1, there will continue to be silence as the child absorbs the sounds of your pattern. In Stage 2, if there is any vocalization, it most likely will not be a musical response that you can identify as being directly related to the pattern you just sang for her. The child has phased through Stage 3 if she vocalizes a musical response that is directly related to the syntax of the tonality in which you are singing patterns, that is, she is likely to vocalize a characteristic pitch of the music she is hearing, such as the dominant or the tonic pitch. If a child consistently responds with her own personal pitch, then she is prepared to learn how to imitate tonal patterns.

At this point, it is crucial that adults do not expect children to imitate exactly tonal Acculturation Patterns, nor should they engage in "drill and practice."

Instead, adults should continue with tonal Imitation Pattern guidance as described on page 27 of the *Guide,* or within any of the tonal Imitation Pattern Activities.

Following are appropriate tonal Acculturation Patterns (Gordon, 1997). Although the patterns are notated in the keyality of D Major and D Harmonic Minor, they should be transposed to the keyality of the song that was sung previous to pattern guidance.

TONAL ACCULTURATION PATTERNS WITHOUT WORDS: STAGES 1 - 3

D Major

D Harmonic Minor

Tables 1.1 through 1.3 summarize the information presented about tonal Acculturation Patterns and pattern guidance for children in the Acculturation type of preparatory audiation.

TABLE 1.1 / ACCULTURATION STAGE 1: TONAL

ACCULTURATION: TONAL Birth to age 2-4: Child engages with little consciousness of the environment.	STAGE 1	ABSORPTION Child hears and aurally collects the sound of music in the environment.

CHILD'S RESPONSES OR REACTIONS TO MUSIC	TEACHER'S INTERACTION WITH CHILD'S RESPONSES
Child turns her head or looks toward music or even watches while hearing the music, but does not make a vocal response. Child sometimes will move during the silences.	Sing three-note, diatonic, tonal Acculturation Patterns while making eye contact with individual children and smiling. Model a deep, full breath preceding each tonal pattern. During tonal pattern guidance, invite a second adult to breathe and echo your diatonic tonal pattern. Do not verbally or physically encourage child to make a response. Be sensitive to child by not continuing pattern guidance too long. Continue with unstructured, informal guidance during tonal Acculturation Pattern guidance and classroom activities. Continue singing tonal Acculturation Patterns and performing music in a variety of tonalities and meters while moving with continuous flow.

TABLE 1.2 / ACCULTURATION STAGE 2: TONAL

ACCULTURATION: TONAL	STAGE 2	RANDOM RESPONSES
Birth to age 2-4: Child engages with little consciousness of the environment.		Child moves and babbles in response, but without relation, to the sounds of music in the environment.

CHILD'S RESPONSES OR REACTIONS TO MUSIC	TEACHER'S INTERACTION WITH CHILD'S RESPONSES
Child begins to participate by babbling sounds and movements that are not coordinated, and with vocal responses that do not resemble the singing in his environment. Child may also perform various movements that seem to be stimulated by, but not necessarily related to, her environment.	Continue with all suggestions in Table 1.1 for Stage 1 of tonal preparatory audiation. Reinforce vocal sounds and movements that young children perform. If a child responds with what you determine to be her personal pitch, turn that pitch into the dominant or tonic of your song and patterns temporarily. Then, perform the same tonal pattern in the original keyality in which you presented the song.

TABLE 1.3 / ACCULTURATION STAGE 3: TONAL

ACCULTURATION: TONAL	STAGE 3	PURPOSEFUL RESPONSES
Birth to age 2-4: Child engages with little consciousness of the environment.		Child tries to relate movement and babble to the sound of music in the environment.

CHILD'S RESPONSES OR REACTIONS TO TONAL PATTERNS	TEACHER'S INTERACTION WITH CHILD'S RESPONSES
Child vocalizes a response that is related to the music in her environment. Child will be responding with a singing voice quality. The response may be characteristic of her personal pitch, or may correspond to the tonality presented, such as the resting tone or the dominant pitch. Child may attempt the adult's pattern, or her own pattern, but not necessarily with an accurate or precise performance.	Introduce structured, informal guidance during tonal Acculturation Pattern guidance and classroom activities. Continue all other suggestions in Table 1.1. Imitate child's vocal responses and continue to sing tonal Acculturation Patterns. Be alert for child's spontaneous performances of a resting tone or dominant pitch, either on its own or within a pattern, which signals you to begin singing perfect 5th and perfect 4th tonal Imitation Patterns to that child. After a child performs a resting tone or dominant pitch, do not drill and practice in expectation that a child will precisely imitate an Acculturation Pattern. Encourage spontaneous songs, chants, and movements created by child. Continue singing tonal Acculturation Patterns and performing music in a variety of tonalities and meters while moving with continuous flow.

TONAL PATTERN GUIDANCE
IMITATION PATTERNS: STAGE 4

Within the Imitation type of preparatory audiation, there are two sets of Imitation Patterns. The first set is sung for a child who is in Stage 4 of preparatory audiation, which means that she has just performed a resting tone or dominant pitch in response to an Acculturation Pattern. The second set is sung for a child who is in Stage 5 of preparatory audiation, and will be described in the next section. *It is appropriate to model continuous flow while children are phasing through Stages 4 and 5 of the Imitation type of preparatory audiation.*

The first set of Imitation Patterns feature the dominant-to-tonic relationship in Major tonality or Harmonic Minor tonality by presenting two-note pitches, either a perfect fifth or a perfect fourth apart, such as "so-do" approached from "so" above and below "do" in Major tonality and "mi-la" approached from "mi" above and below "la" in Harmonic Minor tonality. As with Acculturation Patterns, Imitation Patterns for Stage 4 are preceded with a deep, full breath and are sung with a pleasant singing quality without excessive vibrato. They are performed on neutral syllables with the first consonant of the syllable repeated for each pitch of a pattern. All pitches are of equal duration. Unlike Acculturation Patterns, Imitation Patterns are *not* sung *legato.* Instead, each of the two pitches should be short, with a separation of silence between the two. In this way, it is possible for young children to begin to audiate the separate pitches in the tonal pattern before they attempt to imitate them. Also, because the tonal patterns are no longer entirely diatonic after stage 3, young children will begin to sing arpeggioed tonal patterns with more accuracy and precision.

During Stage 4 of preparatory audiation, a young child begins to learn the process of imitation. As with Stage 3 of preparatory audiation, adults should not expect an exact imitation of the tonal pattern presented. Instead, they should accept any vocal response from a child who is attempting to imitate the adult's pattern. Often, the child's attempt will result in a different tonal pattern from the one the adult presented. It may or may not include the resting tone or the dominant pitch, or it might even be a more precise imitation of the adult's pattern.

In any case, adults should be listening to tonal responses and looking for children who are giving an "audiation stare." This occurs when a young child makes a vocal response, but indicates through her reaction that she realizes that what she performed was not the same as what the adult performed. If children are inaccurately imitating the Imitation Patterns for Stage 4 and do not perform an "audiation stare," adults should continue to engage young children in tonal pattern dialogue by briefly using the child's inaccurate tonal pattern to begin another pattern dialogue for the child to imitate. By using her inaccurate tonal pattern, you are reinforcing the idea that her response was not only acceptable, but a very important one that you would like for her to repeat. Then, you should return to the original tonality and keyality of the tonal patterns as they were presented and present your original tonal Stage 4 Imitation Pattern again. When a child engages in an "audiation stare," this is an indication that she has phased into Stage 5 and the adult should begin singing tonal Imitation and Assimilation Patterns for her.

Following are examples of tonal Imitation Patterns for Stage 4 of preparatory audiation (Gordon, 1997). Although the tonal patterns are notated in the keyality of D Major and G Harmonic Minor tonalities on page 27, these patterns should be transposed to the keyality of the song that was sung previous to pattern guidance. If you are performing songs as notated in the *Guide,* you will notice that the corresponding patterns are written in a range that is appropriate for a young child's initial singing range.

TONAL IMITATION PATTERNS WITHOUT WORDS: STAGE 4

D Major

D Harmonic Minor

Table 2.1 summarizes the information presented about tonal Imitation Patterns and pattern guidance for childen in Stage 4 of the Imitation type of preparatory audiation.

TABLE 2.1 / IMITATION STAGE 4: TONAL

IMITATION: TONAL	STAGE 4	SHEDDING EGOCENTRICITY
Ages: 2-4 to 3-5 years Child participates with conscious thought focused primarily on the environment.		Child recognizes that her movement and babble do not match the sounds of music in the environment.

CHILD'S RESPONSES OR REACTIONS TO TONAL PATTERNS	TEACHER'S INTERACTION WITH CHILD'S RESPONSES
Child will attempt tonal patterns, not necessarily with accuracy, and with no coordination among breathing, moving, and singing. At first, there may be no indication that the child realizes her pattern is different from the model. Child's tonal pattern may contain the resting tone or the dominant pitch. When child realizes that what she is performing is different from the model, she does so with an "audiation stare."	Continue with structured informal guidance during tonal Imitation Pattern guidance and classroom activities. Perform Imitation Patterns that feature the resting tone and a perfect fifth above or a perfect fourth below, if the range of the pattern accommodates child's singing and initial audiation range. Continue to model a deep, full breath preceding each tonal pattern. Encourage the child to respond by changing your facial expressions, using gestures, and moving with continuous flow that emphasizes differences in weight, space, and time. As a child responds inaccurately to your tonal pattern, use her inaccurate pattern to begin a pattern dialogue with her so that she may learn the process of imitation. Return frequently to the original tonal Imitation Patterns. If a child performs an "audiation stare," move to Stage 5. Encourage spontaneous songs, chants, and movements created by child. Continue to perform music in a variety of tonalities and meters while moving with continuous flow.

TONAL PATTERN GUIDANCE
IMITATION PATTERNS: STAGE 5

After a child has responded with an "audiation stare" in Stage 4, which indicates that she is aware that her tonal pattern is not the same as your pattern, she is prepared for Stage 5 of preparatory audiation. Imitation Patterns in Stage 5 feature the tonic and dominant functions of Major and Harmonic Minor tonalities. The patterns are arpeggioed, with the exception of "so" to "fa" in Major tonality and "mi" to "re" in Harmonic Minor tonality.

As with tonal Imitation Patterns in Stage 4, Stage 5 tonal Imitation Patterns are preceded with a deep, full breath and are sung with a pleasant singing quality without excessive vibrato. They are performed using neutral syllables with the first consonant of the syllable repeated for each pitch of a pattern. Each pitch is of equal duration. Each of the pitches in a tonal Imitation Pattern for Stage 5 of preparatory audiation should be short, with a silent separation between each one. In this way, young children will begin to audiate the pitches in the tonal pattern before they attempt to imitate them. Also, because the tonal patterns are no longer entirely diatonic, young children will begin to sing arpeggioed patterns with more accuracy and precision. Three-note patterns should be presented prior to four-note patterns.

The purpose of tonal Imitation Patterns for children who are in Stage 5 of preparatory audiation is to continue to assist each child to teach herself the process of imitation. Her responses to your tonal patterns most likely will not be precise. Use the inaccurate tonal patterns to begin a pattern dialogue so that the child may precisely imitate her own pattern. During Stage 5, you are listening for children who are figuring out the process of imitation and who are beginning to engage in the imitation of tonal patterns with more precision and accuracy. A child's success with more accurate imitation is an indication that she is prepared for Assimilation Pattern Activities and Stages 6 and 7 of pattern guidance. Following are Imitation and Assimilation Tonal Patterns appropriate for Stage 5 of preparatory audiation. Although the patterns are notated in the keyality of D Major and D Harmonic Minor, they should be transposed to the keyality of the song that was sung previous to pattern guidance. It will be helpful to remember that, although the following tonal patterns are used for Stages 6 and 7 as well, you will follow different guidelines for Tonal Pattern Guidance: Assimilation Stages 6 and 7.

TONAL IMITATION AND ASSIMILATION PATTERNS WITHOUT WORDS: STAGE 5

D Major

G Harmonic Minor

Table 2.2 summarizes the information presented about tonal Imitation Patterns and pattern guidance for children in Stage 5 of the Imitation type of preparatory audiation.

TABLE 2.2 / IMITATION STAGE 5: TONAL

IMITATION: TONAL	STAGE 5	BREAKING THE CODE
Ages: 2-4 to 3-5 years Child participates with conscious thought focused primarily on the environment.		Child imitates with some precision the sounds of music in the environment.

TABLE 2.2 / IMITATION STAGE 5: TONAL (continued)

CHILD'S RESPONSES OR REACTIONS TO TONAL PATTERNS	TEACHER'S INTERACTION WITH CHILD'S RESPONSES
Child has indicated that she realized her tonal patterns were different from the adult's. Child is continuing to learn about imitation by engaging in pattern dialogue. Child's tonal patterns may or may not be precisely like the adult's.	Continue structured informal guidance during tonal Imitation Pattern guidance and classroom activities. Administer the tonal portion of *Audie* if the child is three or four years of age, or *Primary Measures of Music Aptitude* if she is five to 10 years of age. Begin monitoring specific and individual differences among children's tonal responses in relation to their developmental tonal aptitudes. Sing arpeggioed tonal Imitation and Assimilation Patterns. Continue to model a deep, full breath preceding each tonal pattern. Continue assisting child in discovering the process of imitation by creating a tonal pattern dialogue using her inaccurate patterns. Frequently return to original tonal patterns. Encourage child to imitate you by using facial expressions, gestures, and movement with continuous flow that include weight, space, and time. Encourage spontaneous songs, chants, and movements created by child. Continue performing music in a variety of tonalities and meters while moving continuous flow.

TONAL PATTERN GUIDANCE
ASSIMILATION: STAGES 6 - 7

A child indicates she is prepared to enter Stage 6 when she has successfully engaged in the imitation of tonal patterns performed by an adult, but without conscious thought. That is, it is apparent to you that a child is not thinking about what she is doing before she does it. She will not be taking a breath before she performs a tonal pattern, for example. You will present the same type of patterns, using the same breathing and singing techniques as you did during Stage 5. *Continue to move your whole body with continuous flow during Assimilation tonal pattern guidance* There will be a difference, however, in the type of activities that you will present and in which the child will engage, as well as a difference in how you will expect her to respond.

In Stage 6 of preparatory audiation, young children are beginning to understand that they are not coordinating their breathing with their singing and moving. While this lack of coordination is obvious to adults in the environment, at no time should any adult tell a child that the tonal patterns she is performing are wrong or that they are not coordinated with her moving and breathing. Instead, adults should model continuous flow and suggest that the children move as they are moving. When children are moving with continuous flow, sing tonal Assimilation Patterns for them and ask them to be your echo. Adults should all be certain to pause before they breathe and sing each tonal Assimilation Pattern for children, because it is by observing an appropriate breathing, moving, and singing model that children are able to teach themselves to coordinate their breathing with their moving and singing.

Please refer back to page 28 for examples of tonal Assimilation Patterns for Stages 6 and 7 of preparatory audiation. Although the patterns are notated in the keyality of D for both Major and Harmonic Minor tonalities, these patterns should be transposed to the keyality of the song that was sung previous to pattern guidance. If you are performing songs as notated in the *Guide,* you will notice that the patterns are written in a range that corresponds with a young child's initial singing range.

Tables 3.1 and 3.2 summarize information about the tonal Assimilation Patterns and pattern guidance for children in the Assimilation type of preparatory audiation.

TABLE 3.1 / ASSIMILATION STAGE 6: TONAL

ASSIMILATION: TONAL	STAGE 6	INTROSPECTION
Ages: 3-5 to 4-6 years Child participates with conscious thought focused on the self.		Child recognizes the lack of coordination between singing, chanting, breathing, and movement.

CHILD'S RESPONSES OR REACTIONS TO TONAL PATTERNS	TEACHER'S INTERACTION WITH CHILD'S RESPONSES
Child engages in the process of imitation, but indicates that she realizes her breathing and moving are not coordinated with her singing by looking at the adult who initiated patterns or at her own parent. After beginning to perform a tonal pattern without a breath, a child will stop herself and begin again, trying to breathe before singing. Through repetition a child will practice moving and singing, but her movements may not be consistently coordinated with her breathing and singing.	Continue structured informal guidance during arpeggioed, tonal Assimilation Pattern guidance and classroom activities. Continue to model a deep, full breath preceding each tonal pattern. Be certain to present all possible arpeggioed tonic and dominant tonal patterns in Major and Harmonic Minor tonalities to children to increase their tonal pattern vocabularies. Encourage children with suggestions such as "move like this," or "watch me." Stand and engage your whole body in continuous, flowing movement. Structure opportunities for repeating activities that emphasize moving, breathing, and performing tonal patterns. At no time tell the child that her patterns are incorrect or that she is not coordinating her breathing and moving with her singing. Encourage spontaneous songs, chants, and movements created by child. Continue to perform music in a variety of tonalities and meters while moving with continuous flow.

RHYTHM PATTERN GUIDANCE

Rhythm patterns and rhythm pattern activities typically are presented in the same tempo and same meter as the chant directly preceding the patterns. The preceding chant places the content of the patterns in a musical context by establishing the meter for children. As described previously, all rhythm patterns are chanted for children with inflection, but without specified pitches. Please refer to *Fireworks,* page 84, or page 32 and 36 of this section for examples of rhythm patterns.

Rhythm pattern guidance requires the teacher to learn two basic sets of patterns.

1. Acculturation Patterns: Stages 1 - 3 of preparatory audiation

2. Imitation and Assimilation Patterns: Stage 4 - 7 of preparatory audiation

A complete description of the types and stages of preparatory audiation and rhythm pattern guidance can be found in *A Music Learning Theory for Newborn and Young Children,* (Gordon, 1997).

There are elements common to rhythm pattern guidance, regardless of the type of patterns you are presenting. Rhythm patterns should be, as mentioned previously, in the same tempo and the same meter as the chant immediately preceding them. To perform rhythm patterns, take a full, deep breath for the duration of one macrobeat. Your first breath should indicate the tempo of the rhythm pattern you are about to present.

TABLE 3.2 / ASSIMILATION STAGE 7: TONAL

ASSIMILATION: TONAL	STAGE 7	COORDINATION
Ages: 3-5 to 4-6 years Child participates with conscious thought focused on the self.		Child coordinates singing with breathing and movement.

CHILD'S RESPONSES OR REACTIONS TO TONAL PATTERNS	TEACHER'S INTERACTION WITH CHILD'S RESPONSES
After child realizes she has not taken a breath before her tonal pattern, she becomes more consistent in her attempts to coordinate breathing and moving with singing. Child continues to improve the accuracy with which she performs tonal patterns.	Continue structured informal guidance during arpeggioed tonal Assimilation Pattern guidance and classroom activities. Continue to model a deep, full breath preceding each tonal pattern. At this time, continue to introduce and repeat activities that encourage child to breathe consistently, such as hopping or jumping before singing and then immediately engage child in moving with continuous flow while she performs tonal patterns. If children are still unable to perform complete tonal patterns while moving with continuous flow, invite them to sing only the resting tone as you present two, then three, then four note patterns to them. Encourage spontaneous songs, chants, and movements created by child. Perform tonal patterns in tonalities other than Major or Harmonic Minor. Make recommendations about formal instruction in music when child has phased through Stage 7 in both tonal and rhythm preparatory audiation.

Rhythm patterns should be performed in an expressive, musical way, one in which inflection is used as when speaking to young children. To increase the expressive quality of your chanting voice, play with combinations of legato and staccato articulation and dynamic contrasts. Use a neutral syllable to perform rhythm patterns, such as "bah" or even sounds that babbling infants and toddlers make spontaneously, such as "yah" or "yeh." Repeat the consonant for each duration in the pattern to articulate the rhythm. Make eye contact with the child to whom you are chanting and smile, just as you would if you were speaking to her. During *all stages* of rhythm pattern guidance, it is appropriate for you and the caregivers to model continuous flow.

After you chant rhythm patterns to a young child, your patterns may be followed by silence. If you are teaching with another adult, or if a caregiver feels com-fortable doing so, she can echo your rhythm pattern. Be certain that the adult also models (or the group of caregivers also model) a full macrobeat breath before chanting, again with an expressive quality that varies in its inflection. When other adults echo your rhythm patterns, it is crucial that they begin their pattern on the first macrobeat following the last macrobeat of your pattern. (This is different from tonal pattern dialogue, during which it is appropriate to have a short, silent pause before the adult breathes and sings.) The adults must model a breath on the final macrobeat of your pattern in order to enter on the first macrobeat after your pattern is completed. The authors recommend providing a simple breath gesture that indicates when adults are to breathe. It is important that you ask other adults sometimes to be silent following your rhythm patterns, as it is often during silences that a child's rhythm responses will occur.

RHYTHM PATTERN GUIDANCE
ACCULTURATION PATTERNS: STAGES 1 - 3

For children who in the Acculturation type of preparatory audition, adults should neither expect nor physically or verbally encourage young children to respond to pattern guidance. To become acculturated in music, fundamentally, is to absorb the syntax - in this case, the meter - of the music being presented. Absorption, not performance is the purpose of using rhythm patterns at this point in a young child's music development.

Rhythm Acculturation patterns are two macrobeats in length, regardless of the meter you are presenting. It is recommended that your rhythm patterns end with either a macrobeat or microbeats, and that the first underlying macrobeat contains more rhythmically active functions, such as divisions or elongations. Macrobeats and microbeats are also appropriate for the first underlying macrobeat. (Please refer to rhythm Acculturation Patterns in this part, notated below.) *During all three stages of the Acculturation type of preparatory audition, it is appropriate for you and caregivers to model continuous flow.*

After you chant rhythm Acculturation Patterns to a young child, your patterns may be followed by silence. If you are teaching with another adult, or if a caregiver feels comfortable doing so, she can echo your rhythm pattern following the suggestions described previously on page 31. If silence follows your pattern, different types of vocal responses will eventually take place while the child is in the Acculturation type of preparatory audition. If the child is in Stage 1, there will continue to be silence as the child absorbs the sounds of your pattern. If the child is in Stage 2, she may vocalize rhythmic sounds that you cannot identify as being directly related to the rhythm pattern you just chanted for her.

A child is in Stage 3 of preparatory audition if she vocalizes a musical response that is directly related to the syntax of the meter or tempo in which you are chanting patterns. That is, if she chants the underlying microbeats of the pattern, or if she consistently responds with movements that reflect the tempo or meter of the pattern, she is prepared to learn how to imitate rhythm patterns and to be phased into Stage 4 of preparatory audition. When a child responds in Stage 3, it is crucial that adults should not expect children to exactly imitate the rhythm Acculturation Patterns through "drill and practice." Instead, adults should continue with rhythm Imitation Patterns as described on pages 34 and 35 of the *Guide,* or within any of the rhythm Imitation Pattern Activities.

Following are appropriate Acculturation Patterns. Although they are notated with quarter-note macrobeats for examples in Usual Duple meter and dotted-quarter note macrobeats for examples in Usual Triple meter, it would have been possible to write patterns that are audiated as being in the same meter using different durations and measure signatures.

RHYTHM ACCULTURATION PATTERNS WITHOUT WORDS: STAGES 1 - 3

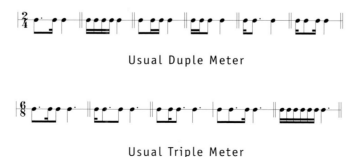

Usual Duple Meter

Usual Triple Meter

Tables 4.1 through 4.3 summarize the information presented about rhythm Acculturation Patterns and pattern guidance for children in the Acculturation type of preparatory audition.

TABLE 4.1 / ACCULTURATION STAGE 1: RHYTHM

ACCULTURATION: RHYTHM	STAGE 1	ABSORPTION
Ages: Birth to 2-4 years Child engages with little consciousness of the environment.		Child hears and aurally collects the sound of music in the environment.

CHILD'S RESPONSES OR REACTIONS TO MUSIC	TEACHER'S INTERACTION WITH CHILD'S RESPONSES
Child turns her head or looks toward music or even watches while hearing the music, but does not make a vocal response. Child sometimes will move during the silences.	Chant two-macrobeat rhythm Acculturation Patterns with expression and conversation-like inflection, mixing staccato and legato articulation and using changes in dynamics. Make eye contact with individual children and smile. Model a deep, full macrobeat breath preceding each rhythm pattern. During pattern guidance, invite another adult to breathe and echo your two-macrobeat rhythm pattern. Observe indications of the variations among each child's personal tempo. Do not verbally or physically encourage child to make a response. Be sensitive to child by not continuing pattern guidance too long. Continue with unstructured, informal guidance during rhythm Acculturation Pattern guidance and classroom activities. Continue performing music in a variety of tonalities and meters while moving with continuous flow.

TABLE 4.2 / ACCULTURATION STAGE 2: RHYTHM

ACCULTURATION: RHYTHM	STAGE 2	RANDOM RESPONSES
Ages: Birth to 2-4 years Child engages with little consciousness of the environment.		Child moves and babbles in response, but without relation, to the sounds of music in the environment.

CHILD'S RESPONSES OR REACTIONS TO MUSIC	TEACHER'S INTERACTION WITH CHILD'S RESPONSES
Child begins to participate by babbling sounds and movements that are not coordinated with each other, and with vocal responses that do not resemble the chanting in her environment. Child may also perform various movements that seem to be stimulated by, but not necessarily related to, her environment.	Continue with suggestions for Stage 1 of rhythm preparatory audiation. Reinforce vocal sounds and movements that young children perform. If child responds with vocal sounds or movements with what you determine to be her personal tempo, use that tempo to repeat your patterns temporarily. Then, perform the same pattern in the original tempo in which you presented them. Continue with unstructured, informal guidance during rhythm Acculturation Pattern guidance and classroom activities. Continue chanting rhythm Acculturation Patterns and performing music in a variety of tonalities meters while moving with continuous flow.

TABLE 4.3 / ACCULTURATION STAGE 3: RHYTHM

ACCULTURATION: RHYTHM	STAGE 3	PURPOSEFUL RESPONSES
Ages: Birth to 2-4 years Child engages with little consciousness of the environment.		Child tries to relate movement and babble to the sound of music in the environment.

CHILD'S RESPONSES OR REACTIONS TO RHYTHM PATTERNS	TEACHER'S INTERACTION WITH CHILD'S RESPONSES
Child vocalizes a response that is related to the music in her environment. Child will be responding with a chanting voice quality. Child's response may be characteristic of her personal tempo, or may correspond to the meter presented, such as moving to or chanting to the underlying microbeat. Child may attempt the adult's pattern, or her own pattern, but not necessarily with an accurate or precise performance.	Introduce structured, informal guidance during rhythm Acculturation Pattern guidance and classroom activities. Continue to model a deep, full macrobeat breath preceding each rhythm pattern. Imitate child's purposeful responses and continue to chant rhythm Acculturation Patterns. Be alert for child's vocal or physical spontaneous performances of underlying microbeats, which signals you to begin chanting four-macrobeat Imitation Patterns for that child. Do not drill and practice in expectation that a child will precisely imitate an Acculturation Pattern. Encourage spontaneous songs, chants, and movements created by child. Continue performing music in a variety of tonalities and meters while moving with continuous flow.

RHYTHM PATTERN GUIDANCE
IMITATION PATTERNS: STAGES 4 - 5

Children who have rhythmically phased into Stage 4 of preparatory audiation show an awareness of macrobeats and microbeats through vocal and/or movement responses, but are not able and should not be expected to perform either with precision. It is for that reason, in part, that rhythm Imitation Patterns become four macrobeats in length. Also, because patterns are longer, children are less likely to imitate more precisely by chance or to memorize patterns after repeated hearings of four-macrobeat patterns.

There is a recommended structure for four-macrobeat patterns used during the Imitation type of preparatory audiation. Please refer to the examples of rhythm Imitation and Assimilation Patterns on page 36 of this section as you read the following descriptions. (The rhythm patterns used for the Imitation and Assimilation types of preparatory audiation are the same.) Regardless of meter, on the first and second underlying macrobeats of rhythm patterns, chant macrobeats, microbeats, or combinations of macrobeats and microbeats. The third underlying macrobeat should contain a division or elongation of a microbeat, and on the final underlying macrobeat, chant only a macrobeat.

The purpose of presenting rhythm patterns in Stage 4 of preparatory audiation is to provide children with the opportunity to discover what the process of imitation actually is. For that reason, when a child inaccurately imitates your four-macrobeat rhythm pattern, use her inaccurate rhythm pattern to try to engage her in another pattern dialogue. This reinforces her response as being not only acceptable, but important, and that may encourage her to imitate accurately the inaccurate pattern. Return to your original rhythm pattern in the original tempo and meter it was presented, being certain to present a variety of four-macrobeat patterns to her. Continue to provide her with opportunities for imitating rhythm patterns until she gives an "audiation stare," which, as described during tonal pattern guidance (page 26), will indicate she realizes that what she is chanting is not the same as what you are chanting. At this point, she is ready to be phased into Stage 5 of preparatory audiation, and you will begin observing her responses.

The purpose of rhythm Imitation Patterns for children who are in Stage 5 of preparatory audiation is to continue to assist a child to teach herself the process of imitation. Her responses to your patterns may not be precise, in which case, you should repeat her inaccurate imitation of your rhythm pattern. Immediately chant two sets of two microbeats in Usual Duple meter or two sets of three microbeats in Usual Triple meter in the tempo you were originally performing, in order to re-establish tempo and meter for the child. Then, repeat the rhythm pattern you originally presented to the child. Remember to present a variety of rhythm Imitation and Assimilation Patterns to her.

Adults should be listening for children who are figuring out the process of imitation and who are beginning to engage in imitation of rhythm patterns with more precision and accuracy. A child's success with more accurate imitation is an indication that she is prepared for Assimilation Pattern Activities and Stages 6 and 7 of rhythm pattern guidance.

Examples of appropriate rhythm Imitation Patterns for Stages 4 - 5 of preparatory audiation are shown on page 36. Although the following Imitation Patterns are notated with quarter-note macrobeats for examples in Usual Duple meter and dotted-quarter-note macrobeats for examples in Usual Triple meter, it would have been possible to write patterns that are audiated in the same meter using different durations and measure signatures. Also, please note that, for rhythm pattern guidance, rhythm patterns appropriate for use in the Imitation type of preparatory audiation are appropriate for use in the Assimilation type of preparatory audiation. Activities you present to children, and their responses, in the Assimilation type of preparatory audiation, however, will not be the same as for the Imitation type of preparatory audiation.

RHYTHM PATTERN GUIDANCE
ASSIMILATION: STAGES 6 - 7

A child indicates she is prepared to enter Stage 6 when she has successfully engaged in the imitation of rhythm patterns (performed by an adult) with some precision, but without conscious thought. That is, it is apparent to the adult that a child is not thinking about what she is doing before she does it. She will not be taking a breath before she performs a rhythm pattern, for example. At this point, the type of rhythm pattern you will present to the child is not different. Instead, there will be a difference in the type of activities you will present and in which the child will engage, as well as your expectations when observing the child's responses.

The recommended structure for four-macrobeat patterns used during the Assimilation type of preparatory audiation is the same as described for rhythm patterns in the Imitation type of preparatory audiation. It is best to refer to the examples of Imitation and Assimilation Patterns on page 36 of this section as you read the descriptions that follow. On the first and second underlying macrobeats of the patterns, regardless of the meter, use macrobeats, microbeats, or combinations of macrobeats and microbeats. The third underlying macrobeat should contain a division or elongation of a microbeat, and on the final underlying macrobeat, you should chant only a macrobeat.

As with Imitation Patterns, Assimilation Patterns are preceded by a deep, full breath that is one macrobeat in duration. The breath before the first rhythm pattern should indicate the tempo in which the pattern will be performed. Rhythm patterns are performed on neutral syllables with the first consonant of the syllable repeated for each duration of the pattern.

In Stage 6 of preparatory audiation, young children are beginning to realize that they are not coordinating their breathing with their chanting and moving. While this lack of coordination is obvious to adults in the environment, at no time should an adult tell a child that patterns she is performing are wrong or that the patterns are not coordinated with her moving and breathing. Instead, adults should model continuous flow and suggest that the children move as the adults are moving. When children are moving with continuous flow, chant Assimilation Patterns and ask them to be your echo. Adults should be certain to model a full macrobeat breath before they chant Assimilation Patterns for children. It is by observing an appropriate model of breathing, moving, and chanting that children are able to teach themselves to coordinate their breathing with their moving and chanting.

RHYTHM IMITATION AND ASSIMILATION PATTERNS WITHOUT WORDS: STAGES 4-7

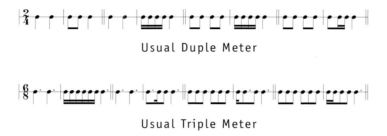

Usual Duple Meter

Usual Triple Meter

Tables 5.1 and 5.2 summarize the information presented about rhythm Imitation Patterns and pattern guidance for children in the Imitation type of preparatory audiation.

TABLE 5.1 / IMITATION STAGE 4: RHYTHM

IMITATION: RHYTHM	STAGE 4	SHEDDING EGOCENTRICITY
Ages: 2-4 to 3-5 years Child participates with conscious thought focused primarily on the environment.		Child recognizes that movement and babble do not match the sounds of music in the environment.

CHILD'S RESPONSES OR REACTIONS TO RHYTHM PATTERNS

Child will attempt rhythm patterns not necessarily with accuracy, and with no coordination among breathing, moving, and chanting. At first, there may be no indication that the child realizes her pattern is different from the model. Child's rhythm pattern may contain accurate microbeat performances. When child realizes that what she is performing is different from the model, she does so with an "audiation stare."

TEACHER'S INTERACTION WITH CHILD'S RESPONSES

Continue with structured informal guidance during rhythm Imitation Pattern guidance and classroom activities.

Perform four-macrobeat Imitation Patterns with expression and conversation-like inflection, mixing *staccato* and *legato* articulation and using changes in dynamics. Continue to model a deep, full macrobeat breath preceding each rhythm pattern. Encourage the child to respond by changing your facial expressions, using gestures, and moving with continuous flow that emphasizes differences in weight, space, and time. As a child responds inaccurately to your rhythm pattern, use her inaccurate pattern to begin a pattern dialogue with her so that she may learn the process of imitation. Return frequently to the original rhythm Imitation Patterns. If a child performs an "audiation stare," move to Stage 5.

Encourage spontaneous songs, chants, and movements created by child. Continue to perform rhythm Imitation and Assimilation Patterns and music in a variety of tonalities and meters while moving with continuous flow.

TABLE 5.2 / IMITATION STAGE 5: RHYTHM

IMITATION: RHYTHM	STAGE 5	BREAKING THE CODE
Ages: 2-4 to 3-5 years Child participates with conscious thought focused primarily on the environment.		Child imitates with some precision the sounds of music in the environment.

CHILD'S RESPONSES OR REACTIONS TO RHYTHM PATTERNS	TEACHER'S INTERACTION WITH CHILD'S RESPONSES
Child has indicated that she realizes when her rhythm pattern is different from the adult's. Child is continuing to learn about imitation by engaging in pattern dialogue. Child's rhythm patterns will not be precisely like the adult's.	Continue structured informal guidance during rhythm Assimilation Pattern guidance and classroom activities. Administer the rhythm portion of *Audie* if child is three or four years of age, or *Primary Measures of Music Aptitude* if she is five to 10 years of age. Begin monitoring specific and individual differences among children's rhythm responses in relation to their developmental rhythm aptitudes.Continue chanting four-macrobeat rhythm Imitation Patterns. Continue to model a deep, full macrobeat breath preceding each rhythm pattern. Continue assisting child in the process of imitation by creating a rhythm pattern dialogue using her inaccurate patterns. Frequently return to original rhythm patterns. Encourage child to imitate you by changing your facial expressions, using gestures, and moving with continuous flow that emphasizes differences in weight, space, and time. Encourage spontaneous songs, chants, and movements created by child. Continue to perform music in a variety of tonalities and meters and move with continuous flow.

Please turn back to page 36 for examples of Assimilation Patterns for Stages 6 and 7 of preparatory audiation. Although the Assimilation Patterns are notated with quarter-note macrobeats in Usual Duple meter and dotted-quarter-note macrobeats in Usual Triple meter, it is possible to write patterns that would be audiated in the same meter using different durations and measure signaturs. Also, please note that, for rhythm pattern guidance, the rhythm patterns appropriate for use in the Assimilation type of preparatory audiation are also appropriate for use in the Imitation type of preparatory audiation. Activities you present to children, and their responses in the Assimilation type of preparatory audiation, however, will not be the same as for the Imitation type of preparatory audiation.

Tables 6.1 and 6.2 summarize information about rhythm Assimilation Patterns and pattern guidance for children in the Assimilation type of preparatory audiation.

TABLE 6.1 / ASSIMILATION STAGE 6: RHYTHM

ASSIMILATION: RHYTHM	STAGE 6	INTROSPECTION
Age: 3-5 to 4-6 years Child participates with conscious thought focused on the self.		Child recognizes the lack of coordination between chanting, breathing, and movement.

TABLE 6.1 / ASSIMILATION STAGE 6: RHYTHM (continued)

CHILD'S RESPONSES OR REACTIONS TO RHYTHM PATTERNS	TEACHER'S INTERACTION WITH CHILD'S RESPONSES
Child engages in the process of imitation, but indicates that she realizes her breathing and moving are not coordinated with her chanting by looking at the adult who initiated patterns or at her own parent. After beginning to perform a rhythm pattern without a full macrobeat breath, child will stop herself and begin again, trying to breathe before chanting. Through repetition, child will practice moving and chanting, but her movements may not be consistently coordinated with her breathing and chanting.	Continue structured informal guidance during four-macrobeat rhythm Assimilation Pattern guidance and classroom activities. Continue to model a deep, full macrobeat breath preceding each rhythm pattern. Be certain to present all possible four-macrobeat rhythm patterns in Usual Duple and Usual Triple meters to children to increase their rhythm pattern vocabularies. Encourage children with suggestions such as "move like this," or "watch me." Introduce continuous flow with pulsations in whole body to microbeats in Usual Duple meter. Structure opportunities for repeating activities that emphasize moving, breathing, and performing rhythm patterns. At no time tell the child that her patterns are incorrect or that she is not coordinating her breathing and moving with her chanting. Assist child with pulsating and chanting simultaneously, encourage her to chant "TAH" to microbeats while pulsating and you chant "BAH" to macrobeats, both in Usual Duple Meter. Encourage spontaneous songs, chants, and movements created by child. Continue to perform music in a variety of tonalities and meters while moving with continuous flow.

TABLE 6.2 / ASSIMILATION STAGE 7: RHYTHM

ASSIMILATION: RHYTHM	STAGE 7	COORDINATION
Age: 3-5 to 4-6 years Child participates with conscious thought focused on the self.		Child coordinates chanting with breathing and movement.

CHILD'S RESPONSES OR REACTIONS TO RHYTHM PATTERNS	TEACHER'S INTERACTION WITH CHILD'S RESPONSES
After child realizes she has not taken a full macrobeat breath before her pattern, she becomes more consistent in her attempts to coordinate her breathing and moving with chanting. Child continues to improve the accuracy with which she performs rhythm patterns.	Continue structured informal guidance during four-macrobeat rhythm Assimilation Pattern guidance and classroom activities. Continue to model a deep, full macrobeat breath preceding each rhythm pattern. Continue to perform four-macrobeat Assimilation Patterns. Introduce and repeat activities that encourage the child to breathe consistently, such as hopping or jumping before chanting. Then immediately engage the child in moving with continuous flow while she performs rhythm patterns. Encourage spontaneous songs, chants, and movements created by child. Perform chants and corresponding rhythm patterns in meters other than Usual Duple and Usual Triple. Make recommendations about formal instruction in music when child has phased through Stage 7 in both tonal and rhythm preparatory audiation.

PART 7

Monitoring Tonal and Rhythm Music Development

Following is a chart that you may use during your classes to record the tonal and rhythm responses of each child. There are many ways you can conduct your record-keeping, but it is recommended that you keep two separate charts, one for tonal responses and one for rhythm responses. The authors suggest that you use a chart to write the name of each child who demonstrates the characteristic response for a given stage in the corresponding box. Writing an "M" next to the name signifies that she demonstrated a response during pattern guidance in Major tonality and "HM" signifies that she demonstrated a response during pattern guidance in Harmonic Minor tonality. A "D" for Usual Duple and "T" for Usual Triple will assist you in keeping rhythm responses separate for each child.

It is possible that a child will progress to another stage in one tonality, but not in another. Similarly, it is possible that a child will progress to another stage in one meter, but not in another. Finally, it is possible for a child to progress tonally to another stage, but not rhythmically, or vice versa. Having another adult who understands pattern guidance as well as the tonal and rhythm responses children characteristically make within the types and stages of preparatory audiation is the most efficient way to monitor music development. As one adult engages children in pattern guidance, the other can quickly record a child's response on the chart.

It is important to remember that children's tonal and rhythm developmental aptitudes fluctuate, which in turn results in fluctuations of their tonal and rhythm responses. Although this is to be expected, do not regress in pattern guidance or pattern activities within a given tonality or meter simply because a child has performed a characteristic response of an earlier stage of preparatory audiation. Instead, maintain the current level of pattern guidance and pattern activities, and patiently wait for her to return to the appropriate level of achievement.

Keeping a record of the responses you observe is easiest if you are working with another adult. If this is not possible, a videotape recording of the classes is a marvelous tool for observing how each child has engaged in music play during a given class. Videotapes are useful in any case, as often it is possible to view responses on tape that you missed during class.

Using a chart such as the one on page 40 for tonal and rhythm pattern responses ensures that you are tracking individuals accurately for the best music guidance you can provide. If possible, make notes to remind you of the variety of movement responses you have observed each child performing: these are valuable in conjunction with tonal and rhythm responses you have observed. Often, children who are not responding by performing movements are also the ones who have not responded with tonal or rhythm responses.

When children are three years of age *and* they have phased to Stage 5 of both tonal and rhythm Imitation, they should be administered *Audie,* a music game for children three and four years of age (Gordon, 1989). *Audie* is a measure of tonal and rhythm developmental aptitude, and is designed for a child and her parent to complete at home. It takes only about 10 minutes to play *Audie,* during which time the child listens to directions given by a man's voice on a cassette recording. He invites the child to play a game. He tells her to listen to *Audie's* special song and to remember it. Then, he asks her to listen to other songs. After each "new" song, *Audie* asks, "Was that my special song?" The child answers, "Yes" or "No." The child's parent, without prompting her child to respond with the correct answer, marks her answer on an *Audie* answer sheet. When the parent returns answer sheets to you, you are able to score them quickly. A child's tonal and rhythm developmental aptitude scores on *Audie* are indications of her potential to achieve in music, and lend insights to providing individual tonal and rhythm guidance for her during *Music Play*. For complete information and instructions for administering *Audie,* consult the test manual.

Invite caregivers to share with you how their children engage in music play outside of a class. Remind caregivers that playing the *Music Play* recording for their children and engaging in activities like the ones used in class are beneficial for the children's music development. Encouraging caregivers and reassuring them that they are capable of providing exemplary models of music and movement play is important. If the caregivers feel insecure about their abilities, they are less likely to engage in music and movement play at home.

The authors recommend that, at the end of the last class, you give each caregiver a simple informative record of what you have observed during the 10 classes. Remind them, if necessary, that you did not make a record of what the caregivers shared with you about their child's responses outside of class over the course of the 10 weeks. Remind them, as well, that there are no "good" or "bad" records, and that there is no "appropriate" age level at which a child should be performing. Finally, emphasize that the environment you have created for children during the 10 weeks has been one in which children have had the opportunity to be immersed in and absorb music and movement play. Outward musical responses, while noted on the chart, are not as important as the listening vocabulary and initial experiences in music and movement play that children have enjoyed.

TABLE 7 / MUSIC DEVELOPMENT CHART

	STAGE 1 Absorb	STAGE 2 Random Response: Observer	STAGE 3 Purposeful Response: Participant	STAGE 4 Audiation Stare	STAGE 5 Engages in Process of Imitation	STAGE 6 Responses not Coordinated	STAGE 7 Coordinated and More Precise
WEEK 1							
WEEK 2							
WEEK 3							
WEEK 4							
WEEK 5							
WEEK 6							
WEEK 7							
WEEK 8							
WEEK 9							
WEEK 10							

PART 8

How to Begin Early Childhood Music Classes

After you have prepared songs, chants, patterns, and are able to move with free and flexible continuous movement, you are ready for the next exciting parts - finding a space, advertising your music classes and planning a *Music Play* session! When deciding how to structure an early childhood music session, the authors recommend accepting no more than 12 children in each class. Each child should be accompanied by at least one caregiver to attend 30-40 minute classes, once or twice each week, for 10 weeks. Separate classes according to age for children birth to 18 months, children 18 months to about 3 years of age, and children 3 and four years of age seem to work well, although mixing the ages also works well, especially if you are working with another adult.

FINDING A SPACE

The classes should be held in a space large enough to accommodate 12 children and their caregivers, and the materials needed for a given class. The space will most comfortable if the floor is carpeted, the room is well-lighted (preferably with natural light), clean, and free of any other materials that potentially may distract children or that potentially may be a safety hazard. It is most convenient if there is a storage space for all of your materials located in the room. Be certain that the room's doorways will not be blocked during class time, that there is a clear display of fire and safety procedures, and that you can easily communicate those procedures and direct persons out of the space in the event of an emergency.

ENROLLMENT FEES

To determine a fee for enrollment, you will need to consider all of the expenses you are likely to incur. Consider expenses such as rental fees for the classroom space, advertising and mailing costs, teaching fees, and materials you will need to purchase to engage in music play. Once you have determined the cost, you might consider a refund policy. Although the necessity to offer a refund is rare, it is best to have decided in advance how you might handle refund requests. If you are self-employed, you will want to consult an accountant about how best to keep track of your business expenses and your income for tax purposes. Finally, you will need to consider insurance for materials or to cover accidents.

ADVERTISING

Advertise your music classes by writing brief articles for local and near-by surrounding city newspapers, church bulletins, local college or university campus newspapers and radio stations, and radio and television stations in your area. This is usually successful in recruiting children and caregivers. Sometimes radio and television stations will conduct an interview with you to be aired as a feature that may act as advertisement, free-of-charge. After one session of early childhood music classes, caregivers' word-of-mouth approval of the program will be your most successful form of advertisement.

CAREGIVER ORIENTATION

Prior to the first music class, an orientation meeting for caregivers only is an excellent format for relaying information to them about what to expect during *Music Play* from both you and the children. An explanation about the music and movement activities, and asking the caregivers to participate in some activities makes it possible for caregivers to begin to understand *why* you will be doing what you do. Videotaped excerpts of classes in progress may be helpful, especially if there are clear examples of the variety of listening, vocal, and movement responses children perform.

During this orientation, it will be useful to emphasize that children will respond in at least as many ways as there are children in the room. What may look like a lack of participation by some children may in fact be the best response: simply listening and absorbing music and movement in the environment. If you choose to present activities from *Music Play* using *A Music Learning Theory for Newborn and Young Children,* you may copy and distribute the Types and Stages of Preparatory Audiation Summary Chart found on page 9 of the *Guide* to provide an outline of the theoretical framework that guides your instruction and your observation of the children's responses. Again, emphasize that *A Music Learning Theory for Newborn and Young Children* is a theoretical framework for observing the music potential and development of each child, rather than precise expectations. Please consult the introductory material on pages 1-44 of the *Guide* as well as *A Music Learning Theory for Newborn and Young Children* for more in-depth information that you might find valuable to communicate to caregivers.

The orientation meeting is also invaluable for communicating details that will help your early childhood music classes run smoothly. Suggest that everyone wear comfortable clothing suitable for free movement and for sitting and lying on the floor. Suggest where to park and, especially if it is an issue, about where not to park; and where to leave strollers. Tell them your preferences for children having or not having toys or snacks during class time; and for having caregivers temporarily take children from the room if they are disrupting the music environment. Finally, a brief description of the fire and safety procedures for the space is also recommended. Although you will speak to caregivers at this meeting, putting the information in writing and distributing copies will help them remember. If caregivers are unable to attend the orientation, offer to mail the information to them instead.

PLANNING A MUSIC PLAY SESSION

To prepare for a 10-week *Music Play* session, it is useful to consider the music and movement content you would like to use for the optimum music development of each child. As you plan your classes, and as you teach your classes, always remember that young children learn by observing and participating in activities that emphasize repetition, variety, and silence. Choose several songs and chants in a variety of tonalities and meters from *Music Play.* Become comfortable with performing those songs and chants. Always move freely when you sing or chant for yourself or others. Then, you will be ready to plan the highest-quality music guidance for the children in your care.

If you are just beginning early childhood music and movement classes, and you are just acquiring a repertoire of movements, songs, chants, and patterns as described in the previous sections, you may be most comfortable making specific plans. List pieces of music to perform, the activities suggested in *Music Play* that accompany the music and, sometimes, even the order you will present the music and activities. While a prepared "order" of music and activities is a good way to begin, the authors have found that as your overall repertoire of movements, songs, chants, and patterns increases, and as you become more experienced and more comfortable teaching, you will rely on the children's music and movement responses to guide your music play, rather than a teacher-centered plan. As such, children's responses are not likely to be isolated responses to an activity on your list, but instead they become the springboard for the dynamic music relationships that exist among music play, music development, and music guidance. This flexible relationship is one of the characteristics that sets *Music Play* apart from more traditional instruction, in that your teaching ultimately and ideally can become not only child-centered, but also spontaneous and improvisational, because you are equipped to engage in music and movement play with any vocal or physical response a child makes.

When sketching out the design for a 30-40 minute class, it is useful to consider all of the repertoire you have secured for yourself. With which tonalities and meters and movements are you prepared to play?

Remember that songs in Major or Harmonic Minor tonality and chants in Usual Duple and Usual Triple are opportunities to intersperse pattern activities as suggested on the second pages of those plans. Then, consider ways to present the variety of tonalities and meters in the music you have selected. Children seem to enjoy playing with the musical differences between two selections when a chant follows a song or vice-versa. Variety also is effective when dramatic changes occur between the types of movements you model from one activity to the next. Finally, children seem to be most playful with the differences that unfamiliar music provides when it is presented after familiar music. The occasional use of songs or chants with words also adds variety.

Preparing 15 songs and chants for a 30-40 minute class should provide you with sufficient material; decide before hand which of them you will not perform should you run short of time. After you have learned how to play with children's music and movement responses, often 8 or 9 songs and chants are enough. As a group, children and caregivers seem to respond favorably to an established music routine for greetings and farewells. The two music routines can be selections with words in which you can include each child's name, but music without words also works well. In the latter case, it is possible to sing or chant a child's name to the final melodic or rhythm pattern, but we do not recommend adding "hello" or "good-bye" words to an entire song that originally does not have words.

TABLE 8 / MUSIC AND MOVEMENT CONTENT

MUSIC CONTENT	MOVEMENT CONTENT	MATERIALS AND INSTRUMENTS TO ENCOURAGE MOVEMENT
VARIETY, REPETITION, SILENCE	**BODY AWARENESS AND**	Empty space for free movement
TONALITY	**CONTINUOUS FLOW**	Chiffon Scarves
Major Tonality	Leading Flow with Individual	Parachute
Major tonal patterns: Acculturation,	Body Parts	Bean Bags
Imitation, Imitation and Assimilation	Continuous Flow in UpperTorso	Story Book, such as *Peter Rabbit*
Minor Tonality	Continuous Flow in Whole Body	Small Trampoline
Minor tonal patterns: Acculturation,	Continuous Flow with Pulsations	Tennis Balls
Imitation, Imitation and Assimilation	**WEIGHT**	Bubble Liquid and Wand
Dorian Tonality	Moving with Strong Flow	Stuffed Animals
Phrygian Tonality	Moving with Gentle Flow	Long Rope for all to hold
Lydian Tonality	**SPACE**	Elastic Band Rings
Mixolydian Tonality	Self and Shared Space Movement	Hula Hoops
Locrian Tonality	Stationary and Locomotor Movement	Tambourines
METER	Body Shapes	Resonator Bells: D
Usual Duple Meter	Levels	Mallets
Usual Triple Meter	Pathways	Hand Drums
Unusual Paired Meter	**TIME**	Rhythm Sticks
Unusual Unpaired Meter	Moving with Quick Flow	Bracelet Jingle Bells
EXPRESSION	Moving with Slow Flow	Finger Cymbals
Style		Triangle and Striker
Dynamics		Egg Shakers
Tempo		Rain Stick
Articulation		Train Whistle
Phrasing		
Form		

The preceding chart is a reminder of the content that is beneficial to mix and match during any 30-40 minute class. For each activity in *Music Play,* the authors have suggested materials they have found useful for engaging children in movements that encourage their music development.

Once you have taught two or more classes, you will find yourself learning about the children and caregivers. You will settle into a pace and routine with which you can work. You will need to examine the music and movement repertoire you have presented and decide how to add new selections and activities,

phase out selections and activities, and during the seventh class or so, re-introduce earlier selections and activities. These decisions are not overwhelming if you remember to include a variety of tonalities and meters in each class. Each group of caregivers and children tends to have favorite *Music Play* songs, chants, and activities, and sometimes groups will not respond to some songs, chants, and activities as well as other groups. As long as you have repertoire to present, you will adapt to group differences very well and, if you engage in *Music Play* by allowing each child's music and movement responses to guide your teaching, you also will adapt well to individual musical differences.

Notes

Notes

Notes

PART 9

Songs, Chants, Tonal Patterns, Rhythm Patterns and Activities

songs without words

Ring the Bells

Edwin E. Gordon

MUSIC CONTENT

Major Tonality

Usual Duple Meter

MOVEMENT CONTENT

FLOW
Continuous Flow
Continuous Flow with Pulsations

MATERIALS NEEDED

Space for free movement

One chiffon scarf per person

Moderate

* Marks the beginning of each phrase.

ACCULTURATION

Perform the song using neutral syllables for the children. Toss a scarf in the air each time you sing the beginning of phrases 1, 2, and 4. Let the scarf flow to the floor as you complete the phrase. Continuously move the scarf through the air as you sing phrase 3. Demonstrate a deep breath before performing the final phrase. Follow this activity with the Acculturation Patterns and Activities suggested on the facing page.

IMITATION

Perform the song as in the Acculturation Activity described above; however, do not sing the final two pitches of the song. Simply audiate and toss a scarf when you reach that pattern. Reinforce tonal responses performed by children who do sing the final pattern by imitating their patterns and then singing *Very nice,* on the resting tone. If the patterns sung by the children are inaccurate, be sure to imitate those inaccuracies, encourage the children to repeat their patterns, and then sing the accurate tonal pattern again. Make eye contact with each child as you are singing her tonal pattern. Follow this activity with appropriate Imitation Patterns and Activities suggested on the facing page.

ASSIMILATION

Perform the song as in the Imitation Activity above, but silently audiate and do not sing out loud each time you toss a scarf. Follow this activity with Assimilation Patterns and Activities suggested on the facing page.

ACCULTURATION PATTERNS / TONAL

ACCULTURATION

STAGE 1:   Child is building a listening vocabulary by hearing music and watching and feeling continuous movement.

STAGE 2:   Child responds with sound or movement babble that is not specifically related to the activity.

STAGE 3:   Child responds with related sound or movement babble during the activity or immediately after a repetition of the activity.

Acculturation Pattern Activity:

Make eye contact with individual children as you take a breath and sing each tonal pattern. Continuously move a scarf as you sing. Pause between each pattern. Notice if individual children vocalize on the dominant pitch or resting tone. Introduce those children to the following Imitation Patterns.

___

IMITATION PATTERNS / TONAL

IMITATION

STAGE 4:   Child becomes aware that her responses are different from the adult's music and movement model.

Imitation Pattern Activity:

Continuously move a scarf as you breathe and sing each tonal pattern. Pause after you sing each pattern and encourage children to imitate your pattern. Expect the children to sing inaccurate tonal patterns and encourage them to repeat those patterns with you. Those children who have performed audiation stares should be phased into Stage 5.

___

IMITATION AND ASSIMILATION PATTERNS / TONAL

IMITATION

STAGE 5:   Child responds with more precise imitation of tonal patterns and movements.

Imitation Pattern Activity:

Perform Imitation and Assimilation Patterns as in the previous Imitation Pattern Activity. Imitate any inaccurate sounds or sound patterns made by individual children. Make eye contact with those children, then sing the dominant pitch followed by the resting tone, and repeat your original pattern.

ASSIMILATION

STAGE 6:   Child develops an awareness of her lack of coordination among her breathing, moving, and singing.

STAGE 7:   Child coordinates her breathing, moving, and singing while imitating tonal patterns precisely.

Assimilation Pattern Activity:

Swing your arms, bend your knees, and breathe before you jump and sing each tonal pattern. Encourage the children to copy your moving, breathing, and singing.

My Mommy is a Pilot

Fast   Edwin E. Gordon

MUSIC CONTENT

Major Tonality

Usual Duple Meter

MOVEMENT CONTENT

FLOW
Continuous Flow
Continuous Fow with Pulsations

MATERIALS NEEDED

Space for free movement

Parachute

One beanbag per person

ACCULTURATION

   Clap the rhythm pattern notated below (and in measures 2 and 10 of the song) several times while making eye contact with individual children. Perform the song several times using neutral syllables for the children and accompany measures 2 and 10 with clapping pattern. Then perform the song without clapping in measures 2 and 10. Give each child approval when he notices the absence of clapping by smiling at her or making eye contact with her. Sway continuously as you sing. Follow this activity with the Acculturation Patterns and Activities suggested on the facing page.

IMITATION

   Perform the song as in the Acculturation Activity described above; however, audiate, but do not sing or clap in measures 2 and 10. Reinforce responses performed by children who do sing or chant patterns in measures 2 and 10 by imitating their patterns and then beginning a pattern dialogue by performing appropriate Imitation Patterns and Activities suggested on the facing page.

ASSIMILATION

   Perform the song using neutral syllables while you and the children hold the edges of a parachute. Bounce the parachute into action on the first macrobeat of measure 1 and let it continuously flow until the first macrobeat of measure 3. Continue this two-measure flow pattern throughout your performance of the song. Follow this activity with Assimilation Patterns and Activities suggested on the facing page.

ACCULTURATION PATTERNS / TONAL

ACCULTURATION

STAGE 1: Child is building a listening vocabulary by hearing music and watching and feeling continuous movement.

STAGE 2: Child responds with sound or movement babble that is not specifically related to the activity.

STAGE 3: Child responds with related sound or movement babble during the activity or immediately after a repetition of the activity.

Acculturation Pattern Activity:

Take a breath and sing each tonal pattern as you continuously move a beanbag through the air. Pause between patterns. Notice if individual children vocalize on the dominant pitch or resting tone. Introduce those children to the following Imitation Patterns.

IMITATION PATTERNS / TONAL

IMITATION

STAGE 4: Child becomes aware that her responses are different from the adult's music and movement model.

Imitation Pattern Activity:

Give each child and caregiver a beanbag. Continuously move your beanbag as you breathe and then drop the beanbag on the floor as you sing the first pitch of each tonal pattern. Make a pause between each tonal pattern and encourage the children to repeat each pattern. Expect the children to sing inaccurate tonal patterns and encourage them to repeat their patterns with you. Those children who have performed audiation stares should be phased into Stage 5.

IMITATION AND ASSIMILATION PATTERNS / TONAL

IMITATION

STAGE 5: Child responds with more precise imitation of tonal patterns and movements.

Imitation Pattern Activity:

Perform Imitation and Assimilation Patterns as in the previous Imitation Pattern Activity. Imitate sounds or sound patterns made by individual children. Make eye contact with those children, then sing the dominant pitch followed by the resting tone and repeat your original pattern.

ASSIMILATION

STAGE 6: Child develops an awareness of her lack of coordination among her breathing, moving, and singing.

STAGE 7: Child coordinates her breathing, moving, and singing while imitating tonal patterns precisely.

Assimilation Pattern Activity:

While each member of the group holds the edges of a parachute, bend at the waist, breathe and raise the parachute. As the parachute begins its descent, sing a tonal pattern and encourage the children to copy your breathing, moving, and singing.

Bumble Bee

Moderate

Edwin E. Gordon

MUSIC CONTENT

Major Tonality

Multimetric: Unusual Paired, Usual Triple

MOVEMENT CONTENT

FLOW
Continuous Flow

WEIGHT
Strong, Gentle

SPACE
Locomotor
High, Medium, Low Levels

TIME
Quick, Slow

MATERIALS NEEDED

Space for free movement

Tambourine

ACCULTURATION

(1) Perform the song while you move with continuous flow. At the end of the song, sing the final pitch of the song again. Pat both hands on the floor. (2) Perform the song as you did in (1). At the end of measure 2, take a deep breath and perform a "Buzzing DO" and tickle a child's tummy. At the end of measure 4, take another breath and perform a "Buzzing SO" and tickle another child's tummy. At the end of measures 6 and 8, take a deep breath, but do not sing anything, just pause as you exhale silently. At the end of measure 10, do not pause at all, but continue singing to the end of the song. At the end of the song, perform a SO to DO buzzing pattern. Follow these activities with Acculturation Patterns and Activities suggested on the facing page.

IMITATION

(1) Perform the song and play a tambourine to each macrobeat. Each time there is a dotted-quarter note in the chant, shake the tambourine for the duration of that note. (2) Pass tambourines around for children to play. Show them how to hold a tambourine, but do not expect them to play accurately as described in the first Imitation Activity. Follow this activity with appropriate Imitation Patterns and Activities on the facing page.

ASSIMILATION

(1) Sing the resting tone for the children, and ask them to sing it. Tell them you will sing a part of the song and, whenever you stop, you will invite them to breathe and sing the resting tone. (2) Tell the children they are the bumble bees in this song. When you begin singing, they are just leaving their last flower for the day, full of nectar. They are to fly very slowly and continuously, using high, medium, and low space, back to their hives while you sing the song once. They must plan to be back in their hives and still by the end of the song. Then, the "bumble bees" can leave their hives first thing in the morning flying quickly and lightly to their first flower, moving continuously during the whole song. Follow these activities with Assimilation Patterns and Activities suggested on the facing page.

ACCULTURATION

> **STAGE 1:** Child is building listening vocabulary by absorbing music and watching and feeling continuous movement.
>
> **STAGE 2:** Child responds with sound or movement babble that is not specifically related to the activity.
>
> **STAGE 3:** Child responds with related sound or movement babble during the activity or immediately after a repetition of the activity.

Acculturation Pattern Activity:

After the last repetition of the song, pause briefly. Then perform Acculturation Patterns for individual children. Be certain to make eye contact with the child to whom you are singing.

IMITATION

> **STAGE 4:** Child becomes aware that her responses are different from the adult's music and movement model.

Imitation Pattern Activity:

After a child has sung the dominant pitch or the resting tone, introduce her to Stage 4 Imitation Patterns. Expect the children to sing inaccurate tonal patterns and encourage them to repeat their patterns with you. When a child performs an audiation stare, phase her into Stage 5.

IMITATION

> **STAGE 5:** Child responds with more precise imitation of tonal patterns and movements.

Imitation Pattern Activity:

Hold hands with a child and move with a gentle, non-rhythmic swimming movement. Sing Imitation and Assimilation Patterns. Imitate sounds or sound patterns made by individual children. Make eye contact with those children, then sing the dominant pitch followed by the resting tone and repeat your original pattern.

ASSIMILATION

> **STAGE 6:** Child develops an awareness of her lack of coordination among her breathing, moving, and singing.
>
> **STAGE 7:** Child coordinates her breathing, moving, and singing while imitating tonal patterns precisely.

Assimilation Pattern Activity:

Perform Imitation and Assimilation Patterns, modeling a breath before each pattern. If children are not able to breathe and sing, encourage them to move with continuous flow and to listen to you as you breathe and sing several patterns.

I Saw a Dinosaur

MUSIC CONTENT

Major Tonality

Usual Duple Meter

MOVEMENT CONTENT

FLOW
Continuous Flow

SPACE
Stationary

MATERIALS NEEDED

Space for free movement

One chiffon scarf per person

Moderate   Edwin E. Gordon

ACCULTURATION

(1) Place a scarf over your head before you begin the song. As you sit or squat near a child, surprise the child by peeking out from under the scarf as you take a breath and begin the song. During the rests, hide again and gently sway or rock side-to-side to the macrobeats. During each repetition of the opening pattern, peek out from under your scarf. (2) Place a child in your lap, facing you. Hold her hands and bounce her every time the pattern MI, RE, DO occurs. During measures 5 through 8, continuously bounce her on the microbeats. During measures 9 through 12, continue to hold the child's hands, swaying while continuously and gently moving her arms in a swimming motion. Upon the return of the opening pattern, resume bouncing the child on the MI, RE, DO pattern. At the end of Acculturation Activities (1) and (2), perform Acculturation Patterns and Activities suggested on the facing page.

IMITATION

During measures 1-8, stand and rock side-to-side to the macrobeat. During measures 9 through the first half of measure 12, stretch up high with alternating hands to the macrobeats. In the second half of measure 12 resume rocking. Encourage children to imitate your movements. Follow this activity with appropriate Imitation Patterns and Activities suggested on the facing page.

ASSIMILATION

Model movement with continuous flow and audiate microbeats in the tempo children expect you to perform *I Saw A Dinosaur*. Then pulsate microbeats with continuous flow in that tempo, inviting children to move like you. Ask them to chant TAH to the microbeats as they pulsate with continuous flow. Chant BAH to macrobeats as you model pulsating microbeats with continuous flow. Follow this activity with Assimilation Patterns and Activities suggested on the facing page.

ACCULTURATION

STAGE 1: Child is building a listening vocabulary by hearing music and watching and feeling continuous movement.

STAGE 2: Child responds with sound or movement babble that is not specifically related to the activity.

STAGE 3: Child responds with related sound or movement babble during the activity or immediately after a repetition of the activity.

Acculturation Pattern Activity:

After a few repetitions of the song, pause briefly. Place a scarf over your head, and peek out to take a breath and perform Acculturation Patterns for individual children. Toss the scarf and let it float down after you have allowed time for children to look and respond before you sing a different pattern. Do not expect each child to noticeably attend to or respond to what you are singing.

IMITATION

STAGE 4: Child becomes aware that her responses are different from the adult's music and movement model.

Imitation Pattern Activity:

After a few repetitions of the song, pause briefly. Then perform patterns notated above for individual children. Be certain to end individual pattern guidance while making eye contact with the child.

IMITATION

STAGE 5: Child responds with more precise imitation of tonal patterns and movements.

Imitation Pattern Activity:

Perform Imitation and Assimilation Patterns as in the previous Imitation Pattern Activity. Imitate any inaccurate sounds or sound patterns made by individual children. Make eye contact with those children, then sing the dominant pitch followed by the resting tone, and repeat your original pattern.

ASSIMILATION

STAGE 6: Child develops an awareness of her lack of coordination among her breathing, moving, and singing.

STAGE 7: Child coordinates her breathing, moving, and singing while imitating tonal patterns precisely.

Assimilation Pattern Activity:

After the last repetition of the song, pause briefly. Then perform Assimilation Patterns for individual children. Be certain to model and encourage continuous movement and taking a breath before singing.

Winter Day

Moderate

Edwin E. Gordon

MUSIC CONTENT

Harmonic Minor Tonality

Unusual Paired Meter

MOVEMENT CONTENT

FLOW
Continuous Flow

COORDINATED BREATHING
Audiating, Moving, Chanting

MATERIALS NEEDED

Resonator Bells: D and mallets

Hand drums

ACCULTURATION

Gather around a parachute. Help adults or children (3 and 4 years or older) securely hold the handles of the parachute. Prior to the beginning of the song, gesture for the whole group to take an audiation breath and lift the parachute. Exhale using a *Shhh* sound and let the parachute float gently to the ground. Repeat the breathing and lifting, this time singing the song using neutral syllables. Follow this activity with Acculturation Patterns and Activities suggested on the facing page.

IMITATION

Place hand drums and resonator bells under the parachute. Continue as in Acculturation Activity above, this time inviting children to play the instruments under the parachute. If adults are holding the parachute, have them stand at the end of the song for a brief time to allow children to explore the instruments. Follow this activity with appropriate Imitation Patterns and Activities suggested on the facing page.

ASSIMILATION

Invite the children to hold the handles of the parachute. Model lifting it at the beginning of each two-measure phrase. Then try the same for each four-measure phrase. Model a *Shhh* sound as in the Acculturation Activity above. Invite the children to coordinate that sound with the duration of each phrase while the parachute falls to the ground as you sing *Winter Day*. Follow this activity with Assimilation Patterns and Activities suggested on the facing page.

ACCULTURATION

STAGE 1: Child is building a listening vocabulary by hearing music and watching and feeling continuous movement.

STAGE 2: Child responds with sound or movement babble that is not specifically related to the activity.

STAGE 3: Child responds with related sound or movement babble during the activity or immediately after a repetition of the activity.

Acculturation Pattern Activity:

After the last repetition of the song, pause briefly. Breathe and lift the parachute as everyone stands. While the parachute is ascending, breathe and perform Acculturation Patterns notated above for individual children. Invite children who are holding the parachute to go under it by singing children's names on the pitches MI and LA.

IMITATION

STAGE 4: Child becomes aware that her responses are different from the adult's music and movement model.

Imitation Pattern Activity:

Repeat the activity as described in the Acculturation Pattern Activity. All children should be standing. If children are holding the parachute, sing Imitation Patterns to an individual holding the parachute. After a child listens or imitates, invite her to play instruments under the parachute.

IMITATION

STAGE 5: Child responds with more precise imitation of tonal patterns and movements.

Imitation Pattern Activity:

Perform Imitation and Assimilation Patterns as in the previous Imitation Pattern Activity. Imitate any inaccurate sounds or sound patterns made by individual children. Make eye contact with those children, then sing the dominant pitch followed by the resting tone, and repeat your original pattern.

ASSIMILATION

STAGE 6: Child develops an awareness of her lack of coordination among her breathing, moving, and singing.

STAGE 7: Child coordinates her breathing, moving, and singing while imitating tonal patterns precisely.

Assimilation Pattern Activity:

Invite children to initiate breathing and lifting the parachute followed by exhaling and performing *Shhh*. Then, sing Assimilation Patterns and encourage all children to breathe and lift the parachute before they sing. Have children individually repeat patterns after you.

The Sled

MUSIC CONTENT

Harmonic Minor Tonality

Usual Triple Meter

ABA Form

MOVEMENT CONTENT

FLOW
Continuous Flow
Continuous Flow with Pulsations

WEIGHT
Strong, Gentle

SPACE
Locomotor

MATERIALS NEEDED

Space for free movement

A   Moderate   Edwin E. Gordon

ACCULTURATION

Perform the song using neutral syllables. Hold a child in your arms as you sing with your cheek pressed to the child's head so that she may feel the vibrations of your singing. Then, perform the song using neutral syllables while performing the following movements. Follow this activity with the Acculturation Patterns and Activities suggested on the facing page.

Section A

Have each caregiver hold a child and continuously sway as the group circles to the right during the first section of the song.

Section B

During the second section of the song, have each caregiver and child continuously sway and move toward the center of the circle during the first phrase and back to their original positions during the second phrase.

Section A

Perform the song and movements as described above in Section A.

IMITATION

Hold hands and create a group circle. Circle to the right and pretend you are walking on eggshells and trying not to break any of them as you sing Section A. Pretend to break all of the eggshells with your feet as you move to the center of the circle for 8 macrobeats and then back to the original circle for 8 macrobeats each time you sing Section B. Encourage the children to move as you are moving. Follow this activity with appropriate Imitation Patterns and Activities suggested on the facing page.

ASSIMILATION

Have the children and caregivers scatter around the room. Hop in place on the first macrobeat of each phrase of Section A as you sing the song. Then swing your arms and jump from place-to-place on the first macrobeat of each phrase of Section B. Continue swinging your arms between jumps. Follow this activity with Assimilation Patterns and Activities suggested on the facing page.

ACCULTURATION PATTERNS / TONAL

ACCULTURATION

STAGE 1: Child is building a listening vocabulary by hearing music and watching and feeling continuous movement.

STAGE 2: Child responds with sound or movement babble that is not specifically related to the activity.

STAGE 3: Child responds with related sound or movement babble during the activity or immediately after a repetition of the activity.

Acculturation Pattern Activity:

Make eye contact with individual children as you take a breath and sing each tonal pattern. Continuously move your arms in a rolling motion as you sing. Pause between patterns. Notice if individual children vocalize on the dominant pitch or resting tone. Introduce those children to the following Imitation Patterns.

IMITATION PATTERNS / TONAL

IMITATION

STAGE 4: Child becomes aware that her responses are different from the adult's music and movement model.

Imitation Pattern Activity:

As you perform the Imitation Activities on the facing page, have the caregivers and children stay close together, holding hands at the center of the circle for the last phrase of Section B. Continuously move as you breathe and sing each tonal pattern. Make a pause between each tonal pattern. Expect the children to sing inaccurate tonal patterns and encourage them to repeat those patterns with you. Those children who have performed audiation stares should be phased into Stage 5.

IMITATION AND ASSIMILATION PATTERNS / TONAL

IMITATION

STAGE 5: Child responds with more precise imitation of tonal patterns and movements.

Imitation Pattern Activity:

Perform Imitation and Assimilatin Patterns as in the previous Imitation Pattern Activity; however, use Imitation Patterns and Assimilation Patterns. Imitate any inaccurate sounds or sound patterns made by individual children. Make eye contact with those children, then sing the dominant pitch followed by the resting tone, and repeat your original pattern.

ASSIMILATION

STAGE 6: Child develops an awareness of her lack of coordination among her breathing, moving, and singing.

STAGE 7: Child coordinates her breathing, moving, and singing while imitating tonal patterns precisely.

Assimilation Pattern Activity:

Swing your arms, bend your knees, and breathe before you jump and sing each tonal pattern. Encourage the children to copy your breathing, moving, and singing.

61

Pennsylvania Dreamin'

Fast

Beth M. Bolton

MUSIC CONTENT

Harmonic Minor Tonality

Usual Triple Meter

MOVEMENT CONTENT

FLOW
Continuous Flow
Continuous Flow with Pulsations

COORDINATED BREATHING
Moving

MATERIALS NEEDED

Space for free movement

Two chiffon scarves per person

ACCULTURATION

Perform the song using neutral syllables. Hold a child in your arms as you sing with your cheek or neck pressed gently to the child's head so that the child may feel the vibrations of your singing. Then, while standing, hold a child in your arms and sway continuously as you sing and travel around the room. Follow this activity with Acculturation Patterns and Activities suggested on the facing page.

IMITATION

While seated, perform the song using neutral syllables and continuously move your shoulders, back, and hips in circular pathways as you and dance with a chiffon scarf. Allow the children to observe you. During the rest at the end of each phrase of the song, take a deep breath and blow your scarf to a child. Follow this activity with appropriate Imitation Patterns and Activities suggested on the facing page.

ASSIMILATION

Give two chiffon scarves to each person. While seated or standing, perform the song using neutral syllables and continuously move your shoulders, back, hips as you and dance with the scarves. Bilaterally bounce your hands to macrobeats as you sing. Never bounce your hands in a place more than once. In this way, you will demonstrate the continuous flow that occurs between macrobeats. Continue to take a deep breath and blow your scarf to a child during the rest after each phrase of the song. Encourage the children to move, breathe, and blow the scarves like you do. Follow this activity with Assimilation Patterns and Activities suggested on the facing page.

ACCULTURATION

STAGE 1: Child is building a listening vocabulary by hearing music and watching and feeling continuous movement.

STAGE 2: Child responds with sound or movement babble that is not specifically related to the activity.

STAGE 3: Child responds with related sound or movement babble during the activity or immediately after a repetition of the activity.

Acculturation Pattern Activity:

Hold a child and press your cheek to her head. Take a breath and continuously sway as you sing each pattern. Pause between each pattern. Notice if individual children vocalize on the dominant pitch or resting tone. Introduce those children to Imitation Patterns.

IMITATION

STAGE 4: Child becomes aware that her responses are different from the adult's music and movement model.

Imitation Pattern Activity:

As you sing each tonal pattern, continuously move your upper body on the first note, and hide your eyes as if playing peek-a-boo on the second note. Have the caregivers in the room imitate you. Expect the children to respond inaccurately and encourage them to sing their inaccurate patterns again. Those children who have performed audiation stares should be phased into Stage 5.

IMITATION

STAGE 5: Child responds with more precise imitation of tonal patterns and movements.

Imitation Pattern Activity:

Breathe and then move continuously and sing each tonal pattern. Pause between patterns. Imitate any inaccurate sounds or sound patterns made by individual children. Make eye contact with those children, then sing the dominant pitch followed by the resting tone, and repeat your original pattern.

ASSIMILATION

STAGE 6: Child develops an awareness of her lack of coordination among her breathing, moving, and singing.

STAGE 7: Child coordinates her breathing, moving, and singing while imitating tonal patterns precisely.

Assimilation Pattern Activity:

Take a breath and toss a scarf as you sing each pattern. Use your body to copy the movement of the scarf as it floats to the floor. Encourage the children to do the same.

Planting Flowers

Fast   Edwin E. Gordon

MUSIC CONTENT

Melodic Minor

Usual Triple Meter

MOVEMENT CONTENT

BODY AWARENESS
Actions associated with planting a garden

FLOW
Continuous Flow

MATERIALS NEEDED

Space for free movement

Story book, such as *Peter Rabbit*

ACCULTURATION

(1) Sing *Planting Flowers* on a neutral syllable while rocking a child in your lap. (2) Read a story to a child, such as *Peter Rabbit* (Beatrix Potter). Periodically stop reading, and sing the song once through while the child enjoys the illustrations on the page you were reading. Follow these activities with Acculturation Patterns and Activities suggested on the facing page.

IMITATION

Improvise a story about Spring and making preparations to plant a garden. Decide with the children whether to plant flowers or vegetables, or both. Begin with moving your bodies like the melting snow on the warming earth. Move as you would to dig the soil, to sew the seeds, and to water the soil. Then move like plants growing in the sunshine. Finally, pretend to pick the flowers or vegetables that have grown in your garden. Sing the song each time, using continuous flow to act out each movement. If children can suggest parts of the story or actions to perform, incorporate their ideas, too. Follow this activity with appropriate Imitation Patterns and Activities suggested on the facing page.

ASSIMILATION

(1) Repeat the activity as described in the Imitation Activity above. Sometimes sing the last two measures aloud as you continue to perform the actions, and other times, silently audiate the last two measures as you move. Invite individual children to finish the song by giving them a "breathe and sing" gesture. (2) Tell children you want them to finish singing the song any way they would like. You will sing almost the whole song and give each child who would like a turn a "breathe and sing" gesture to complete the song. Model continuous movement throughout. Follow either activity with Assimilation Patterns and Activities suggested on the facing page.

ACCULTURATION PATTERNS / TONAL

ACCULTURATION

STAGE 1:   Child is building a listening vocabulary by hearing music and watching and feeling continuous movement.

STAGE 2:   Child responds with sound or movement babble that is not specifically related to the activity.

STAGE 3:   Child responds with related sound or movement babble during the activity or immediately after a repetition of the activity.

Acculturation Pattern Activity:

After a few repetitions of the song, pause briefly. Then perform the patterns for individual children. Be certain to end individual pattern guidance by making eye contact with the child to whom you are singing.

IMITATION PATTERNS / TONAL

IMITATION

STAGE 4:   Child becomes aware that her responses are different from the adult's music and movement model.

Imitation Pattern Activity:

Continue performing the action for the improvised story described in the Imitation Activity on the previous page, and invite children who are ready to imitate the patterns above. Tell the children they are planting music patterns during their music play, and pretend to plant as you breathe and sing a pattern.

IMITATION AND ASSIMILATION PATTERNS / TONAL

IMITATION

STAGE 5:   Child responds with more precise imitation of tonal patterns and movements.

Imitation Pattern Activity:

Perform Imitation and Assimilation Patterns as in the previous Imitation Pattern Activity. Imitate any inaccurate sounds or sound patterns made by individual children. Make eye contact with those children, then sing the dominant pitch followed by the resting tone, and repeat your original pattern.

ASSIMILATION

STAGE 6:   Child develops an awareness of her lack of coordination among her breathing, moving, and singing.

STAGE 7:   Child coordinates her breathing, moving, and singing while imitating tonal patterns precisely.

Assimilation Pattern Activity:

Invite the children to move their whole bodies with continuous flow and audiate as you sing Imitation and Assimilation patterns. Then, invite individual children to echo your patterns while moving with continuous flow. Provide "breathe and sing" gestures to assist them with singing as they move.

Goldfish

Moderate   Beth M. Bolton

MUSIC CONTENT

Dorian Tonality

Usual Triple Meter

MOVEMENT CONTENT

FLOW
Continuous Flow
Continuous Flow with Pulsations

SPACE
High, Medium, Low Levels

MATERIALS NEEDED

Space for free movement

Small trampoline

Two tennis balls per person

ACCULTURATION

Place one or two children on a small trampoline that is low to the ground. Allow other children to sit on the floor and hold on to the edges of the trampoline. Sway and bounce your hands to microbeats as you sing the song. If a child begins to bounce or pat her hands repeatedly in a tempo that is different from yours, copy her movement in her personal tempo and improvise short rhythm chants in her tempo using neutral syllables. Then, return to your original tempo as you sing the song and bounce again. Try not to bounce in the same place twice so that you will demonstrate continuous flow as you bounce.

IMITATION

Have the group sit knee-to-knee in a circle. Give each person 2 tennis balls. Sing the song and demonstrate how to give the tennis balls smooth continuous rides through high, medium, and low space. Invite everyone to move like you do. Roll the balls across the circle at the end of melody, and let each child gather two new balls during the introductory phrase. Repeat the entire activity several times.

ASSIMILATION

Have the group stand and give very smooth rides to the tennis balls as you sing. Encourage the children and caregivers to give interesting rides by exploring the space that is high, medium, or low. To encourage creativity, demonstrate smooth rides and ask the children and caregivers to move differently from you. For instance, if you are giving rides that are low, the children and caregiver could move any place except low.

Dancing

Moderate   Edwin E. Gordon

MUSIC CONTENT

Dorian Tonality

Usual Duple Meter

MOVEMENT CONTENT

FLOW
Continuous Flow

SPACE
Stationary

MATERIALS NEEDED

Space for free movement

Two chiffon scarves per person

ACCULTURATION

(1) Perform the song on a neutral syllable while moving with continuous flow. Draw circular pathways with your shoulders, back, and hips. Use scarves if you would prefer. (2) Assist a toddler to stand on your feet/shoes. Hold her hands and "dance" to macrobeats while you sing. If she is too young for this, bounce her on your knees to macrobeats while you sing.

IMITATION

Repeat activities (1) and (2) above. Then stand in self space to perform continuous flow, with or without scarves, using twisting, bending, and bouncing movements as you sing. Invite children to move as you are moving.

ASSIMILATION

Invite pairs of children to hold hands with each other and rock side-to-side with their arms and feet wide apart, shifting their weight to each macrobeat. Perform the song several times as you take turns being partners with different children. Let them lead the rocking to determine whether they are coordinating their movement with the music. The wider their arms and feet are spread, the more easily they will rock to the macrobeats.

Jumping

MUSIC CONTENT
Dorian Tonality
Usual Triple Meter

MOVEMENT CONTENT
FLOW
Continuous Flow
SPACE
Stationary, Locomotor
COORDINATED BREATHING
Audiating, Moving, Singing

MATERIALS NEEDED
Space for free movement

Moderate   Alison M. Reynolds

ACCULTURATION

Perform the song on a neutral syllable while moving with continuous flow. After two repetitions of the song, stop singing, but continue the flowing movements. Repeat the song and activity. Make eye contact with individual children during the singing and the silence.

IMITATION

When many children in the group have begun to imitate your flowing movements, model swinging movements as you stand in stationary self space. The movements should be like those used as one prepares to jump from one place to another. The swinging movement begins by bending your knees and bringing your arms up in front of you as you take a breath before you begin the song. When you sing the first macrobeat, your arms swing down, and your knees bend slightly. Continue this movement to every other macrobeat as you sing the song. Although you are being specific about how and when you move, do not expect children to imitate your movements precisely.

ASSIMILATION

(1) Swing your arms, taking a breath as your arms swing up in front of you. Let out the breath as your arms fall, and your knees bend slightly. Pause, and then repeat this movement. Ask children to imitate your movement. Then, swing your arms again and complete a jump in which you travel a distance. Be certain that both feet leave the floor at the same time and land at the same time. Finally, sing the song, modeling jumping with full arm swings. The two jumps during the song should land on the downbeats of measures one and five. Encourage the children to breathe and jump as you are doing. (2) Prepare a jump with a breath, arm swing, and knee bend. When you land, sing the resting tone. Have children practice coordinating their breathing, moving, and singing. Invite them to breathe and jump as in (1), this time singing the resting tone when they land. Jump with them, singing the melody *Jumping* with their resting tone accompaniment.

Ocean Waves

Moderate   Wendy H. Valerio

ACCULTURATION

Perform the song using neutral syllables. Hold a child in your arms and rock and sway around the room.

IMITATION

While seated, perform the song using neutral syllables as you continuously rock from side-to-side. Perform the song again and rock from front-to-back. Then, ask children to stand behind caregivers and to gently rock the caregivers from front-to-back by holding on to their shoulders.

ASSIMILATION

Have each caregiver face one or two children while seated on the floor. Give each child one rhythm stick. Have each child and caregiver hold the stick horizontally and pull back and forth in a rowing motion as you sing the song. If one caregiver is working with two children, the caregiver may hold a rhythm stick in each hand, one for each child.

MUSIC CONTENT

Dorian Tonality

Usual Triple Meter

MOVEMENT CONTENT

FLOW
Continuous Flow
Continuous Flow with Pulsations

SPACE
Stationary

MATERIALS NEEDED

Space for free movement

One rhythm stick per child

Country Dance

MOVEMENT CONTENT

FLOW
Continuous Flow

WEIGHT
Strong, Gentle

SPACE
Stationary, Locomotor
Pathways
Direction

COORDINATED BREATHING
Audiating, Moving, Singing

MATERIALS NEEDED

Space for free movement

Moderate   Beth M. Bolton

ACCULTURATION

Pair children with each other, or pair a caregiver with his child. Have each pair face each other, hold hands, and perform a gentle American crawl swimming movement together while you sing *Country Dance*. If you are cradling an infant, gently rock forward and backward or side-to-side as you sing.

IMITATION

(1) Invite children to walk in self space as you sing. Model straight and curvy pathways as you sing and walk to macrobeats. Encourage children not to follow you, but to walk in directions different from each other. (2) Hold hands and perform a circle dance. Move to the left for 8 macrobeats, then to the right for 8 macrobeats. On the next repetition of the song, move to the center of the circle for 8 macrobeats and then out to the original circle for 8 macrobeats. If a child does not want to join the circle, do not force her to do so. As long as she is safe and not disturbing the music, continue to move and sing.

ASSIMILATION

(1) Prepare a jump with a breath and an arm swing. Begin the first phrase of the song when you land. On the last macrobeat of each four-measure phrase, prepare another jump. (The two times you jump, you will prepare the jump on a rest.) Do not expect children to sing the song, but ask them to imitate your jumping. (2) When the children have coordinated their jumping, invite them to sing the resting tone both times they land. Ask them to breathe, jump, and sing. Continue to model the jumps at the correct times as you sing the melody and listen to their resting tone accompaniment.

Red Umbrella

Moderate   Edwin E. Gordon

ACCULTURATION

Perform the song using neutral syllables while moving with continuous flow. After several repetitions, add a gracious *ritard* in the last measure and do not sing the last note (resting tone). As you *ritard,* slow your flowing movement, and when you stop singing, continue to flow but help continue the silence by not talking. When some motion and noise begins, breathe and sing the resting tone.

IMITATION

(1) Perform the song several times as you did for the Acculturation Activity. Continue to flow, singing measures 1 and 2 and then silently audiating measures 3 and 4. Sing the remainder of the song as you flow. Encourage children to imitate your movements. (2) Repeat the flowing movements as described in (1), this time using a scarf. When you silently audiate measures 3 and 4, toss the scarf in the air. Pick up the scarf and continue to flow, using high, medium, and low levels in space as you finish singing the song.

ASSIMILATION

Perform the song several times as you did for the Acculturation Activity. Then, distribute wrist jingle bells. Place a bracelet jingle bell on each wrist and ask the children to do the same. Show them how to continuously flow so that the bells do not jingle. Then, pulsate the microbeats so the children can hear the bells jingle. Ask the children to move like you do. Perform the song, moving once with continuous, non-pulsating flow, and then a second time with continuous flow with pulsations to the microbeats. Be certain to put each microbeat movement in a different space as you move with pulsating flow.

MUSIC CONTENT

Dorian Tonality

Unusual Unpaired Meter

Ritard

MOVEMENT CONTENT

FLOW
Continuous Flow

SPACE
High, Medium, Low Levels

TIME
Quick, Slow

MATERIALS NEEDED

Space for free movement

One chiffon scarf per person

Two bracelet jingle bells per person

Albany

Beth M. Bolton

MUSIC CONTENT

Mixolydian Tonality

Multimetric: Usual Triple, Usual Duple

MOVEMENT CONTENT

FLOW
Continuous Flow

COORDINATED BREATHING
Audiating, Moving, Singing

MATERIALS NEEDED

Two chiffon scarves per person

ACCULTURATION

(1) Perform the song on a neutral syllable while moving with continuous flow. (2) After several repetitions of the song, give each child and adult one scarf for each hand. Perform the song while moving your whole body with continuous flow, making the scarves flow in the space above you, behind you, and all around you. Some children will move in their own ways in response to your movement and music. Observe their movements, and imitate them during a repetition of the song. Do not ask children to move like you. Instead, give them an opportunity to observe your movements and music and to notice your imitation of their movements.

IMITATION

Give each child one scarf. Model continuous flow with your whole body as you move with the scarf. At the end of the first phrase (measure 8), prepare the next phrase by taking a breath. At the beginning of measure 9, toss your scarf up high. From measure 13 to the end of the song, move your whole body with continuous flow without the scarf. Pause after each repetition of the song and pick up your scarf before you resume singing. Encourage children to imitate your movements.

ASSIMILATION

Sing the resting tone (E) for the children. Model a breath gesture and invite the children to sing. Ask them to audiate that sound (resting tone) and perform continuous flowing movements while you sing. Tell them that, whenever you stop singing the song, you will invite them to breathe and sing the sound and move by giving them a "breathe and sing" gesture. Begin singing the song, but stop each time a phrase ends on the resting tone or another note from the tonic function (SO, TI, or RE). After a very brief pause, invite the children to breathe and sing the resting tone. Then, resume your singing. Occasionally, stop singing as described, but leave a silent space without giving the gesture before you resume singing. Children should continue moving, but should not sing if you do not give the gesture.

Good-Bye

Moderate   Beth M. Bolton

MUSIC CONTENT

Phrygian Tonality

Usual Triple Meter

MOVEMENT CONTENT

FLOW
Continuous Flow

SPACE
Stationary

COORDINATED BREATHING
Audiating, Moving, Singing

MATERIALS NEEDED

Space for free movement

ACCULTURATION

(1) If holding an infant, sing the song on neutral syllables while rocking a child from side-to-side. If standing, shift your weight from foot-to-foot, as well as twist your upper torso as you rock. This will create the fullest rocking movement in your body. If the child is awake, keep steady eye contact and smile. (2) Sing the song while moving with continuous flow. Keep eye contact with children and use facial expressions to engage them. Each time you complete the song, insert a long, silent pause. Cease movement during the pauses.

IMITATION

Sing the song and move as you did in the second Acculturation Activity. Encourage children to imitate your movements. At the end of the song, sing the patterns notated below for individual children who have performed tonal responses in Stage 3 of preparatory audiation. Be certain to breathe before you sing each pattern. If children respond with different patterns, imitate their patterns and sing your pattern again. Sing *Goodbye* again to re-establish tonality, and then sing patterns to another child. If children do not respond at all, ask caregivers or a second teacher to sing patterns after you. If a child is able to imitate the pattern, move to the Assimilation Activities below.

ASSIMILATION

(1) If some children are accurately imitating the patterns notated in the Imitation Activity, give them a breath gesture and model breathing to invite them to sing the pattern that starts the song. Prepare them for breathing and singing. (2) To assist a child in coordinating her breathing and singing, hold her hands and move with continuous, swimming movements as she sings and listens. This time, your head and eyes must indicate when she is to breathe and sing the pattern that begins the song.

Stirring Soup

Moderate   Wendy H. Valerio

MUSIC CONTENT

Phrygian Tonality

Unusual Paired Meter

MOVEMENT CONTENT

FLOW
Continuous Flow

WEIGHT
Strong, Gentle

SPACE
Stationary

TIME
Quick, Slow

MATERIALS NEEDED

Space for free movement

ACCULTURATION

Sing the song for the children using neutral syllables as you sit and move your shoulders in continuously flowing pathways. Sometimes move your shoulders quickly, and sometimes move your shoulders slowly, but do not vary the tempo of your singing.

IMITATION

(1) Sing the song for the children using neutral syllables as you stand and rock to macrobeats. Encourage children to stand and rock, but do not expect them to rock to macrobeats with accuracy. Demonstrate a complete shifting of weight by lifting one foot off the floor each time you move from side-to-side. (2) Have each child and caregiver be seated and give each a rhythm stick. Sing the song for the children as you pretend to stir a big pot of soup. Move continuously and fluidly. Stir with one hand and then with the other. Pretend you are stirring broth. Be careful not to splash or spill. With each repetition of the song, have the children choose an ingredient to add to your soup. Chop, slice, or dice each ingredient using combinations of quick, slow, strong, and gentle movements. Let the children be your movement guides. Finally, use all of your strength to stir the thick soup as you sing.

ASSIMILATION

Sing the song for the children using neutral syllables as you stand and swing your arms backward and forward. Raise your hands high above your head as you take a deep breath before the first macrobeat of the song. Allow your knees to bend slightly with each swing. Encourage the children to move like you are moving as you sing.

Daydreams

Slow   Edwin E. Gordon

MUSIC CONTENT

Locrian Tonality

Usual Duple Meter

MOVEMENT CONTENT

FLOW
Continuous Flow
Continuous Flow with Pulsations

TIME
Quick, Slow

COORDINATED BREATHING
Audiating, Moving, Chanting

SPACE
High, Medium, Low Levels

MATERIALS NEEDED

Space for free movement

One chiffon scarf per person

ACCULTURATION

Sing the song using neutral syllables as you rub a child's back. Take a big breath between each phrase of the song.

IMITATION

Give each person a chiffon scarf. Sing the song using neutral syllables and demonstrate a scarf dance as you sing. Encourage the children to make their scarves dance as well. Demonstrate some movements that are very quick and flowing and some movements that are very slow and flowing. Occasionally toss the scarves in the air and use your body to copy their flowing movements to the floor.

ASSIMILATION

(1) Give each person a chiffon scarf. Sing the song using neutral syllables and demonstrate a continuous and circular scarf dance through high, medium, and low space. Encourage the children to make their scarves dance, too. Then, have the children pulsate microbeats as they continuously move and chant BAH to each macrobeat as you continue to sing the song. (2) After completing the song, take a big breath and toss your scarf high as you exhale, and flow to the ground with your body. Encourage the children to do the same. Then, repeat the entire activity.

chants

without

words

Follow Me!

Moderate

Edwin E. Gordon

ACCULTURATION

(1) Perform the chant using neutral syllables. While seated, demonstrate continuous flow with your upper body using your torso, shoulders, arms, and hips. Draw imaginary circles with these body parts as you chant. (2) Demonstrate the use of one type of weight by sometimes moving as if you are in a big puddle of thick mud. Be strong. Demonstrate the use of another type of weight by sometimes moving as if you are in a big bowl of feathers. Be gentle. Make eye contact with individual children as you perform. Repeat several times. Follow each activity with Acculturation Patterns and Activities suggested on the facing page.

IMITATION

(1) Perform the chant using neutral syllables while demonstrating continuous flow as in the previous Acculturation Activity. Pat the floor simultaneously with both hands (bilateral movement) as you perform the final measure of the chant. To reinforce continuous flow, never pat in the same place twice. (2) Perform the chant as in the previous Imitation Activity. When performing the final measure do not chant out loud. Rather, audiate the final measure of the chant and bilaterally pat the floor with both hands. Follow each activity with Imitation Patterns and Activities suggested on the facing page.

ASSIMILATION

(1) Perform the chant using neutral syllables while demonstrating continuous movement as in the Acculturation and Imitation Activities. Have pairs of children or pairs of children and caregivers bilaterally hold hands and pretend to swim continuously as you chant. Tell them to move as if they are in a big puddle of thick mud. Then tell them to move carefully as if they are in a big bowl of feathers and repeat the chant. (2) Perform the chant while demonstrating continuous movement as in the Acculturation and Imitation Activities. Have pairs of children or pairs of children and caregivers bilaterally hold hands, swim continuously, and pulse macrobeats while chanting TAH to each microbeat as you perform the chant. Follow each activity with Assimilation Patterns and Activities suggested on the facing page.

MUSIC CONTENT
Usual Duple Meter

MOVEMENT CONTENT
FLOW
Continuous Flow
Continuous Flow with Pulsations

WEIGHT
Strong, Gentle

COORDINATED BREATHING
Audiating, Moving, Chanting

MATERIALS NEEDED
Space for free movement

ACCULTURATION

STAGE 1: Child is building a listening vocabulary by hearing music and watching and feeling continuous movement.

STAGE 2: Child responds with sound or movement babble that is not specifically related to the activity.

STAGE 3: Child responds with related sound or movement babble during the activity or immediately after a repetition of the activity.

Acculturation Pattern Activity:

Chant each pattern and have caregivers repeat after you. Sometimes sound strong, and sometimes sound gentle. Take a breath and then move continuously as you chant each pattern. Make eye contact with individual children during each pattern you chant.

IMITATION AND ASSIMILATION PATTERNS / RHYTHM

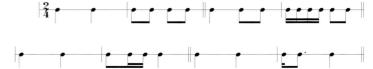

IMITATION

STAGE 4: Child becomes aware that his responses are different from the adult's music and movement model.

STAGE 5: Child responds with more precise imitation of rhythm patterns and movements.

Imitation Pattern Activity:

Chant each pattern and have caregivers and children repeat after you. Breathe before you chant and move continuously as you chant each pattern. Listen to the patterns chanted by the children. Imitate a child's inaccurate response and non-verbally encourage a chanting dialogue with him using his inaccurate pattern. Continue chanting Imitation and Assimilation Patterns for the child until he performs an audiation stare, at which time, he should be phased into Stage 5. For children who are in Stage 5, the adult imitates the inaccurate rhythm pattern responses made by the child, then performs two sets of microbeats in Usual Duple meter in the original tempo that patterns were presented, repeats the original rhythm pattern and non-verbally encourages the child to imitate it.

ASSIMILATION

STAGE 6: Child develops an awareness of his lack of coordination between his breathing and moving, and breathing and chanting by continuously moving and pulsating microbeats as the teacher chants BAH to macrobeats. Then, while performing the same type of movement, the child imitates the rhythm patterns chanted by the teacher.

STAGE 7: Child coordinates his breathing, moving, and chanting while imitating rhythm patterns precisely.

Assimilation Pattern Activity:

Swing your arms from back-to-front as you breathe before delivering each pattern. Allow your arm swings to propel you into a forward jump, landing on the first macrobeat of each pattern. Pretend to swim as you chant the second, third, and fourth macrobeats of each pattern. Have the children and caregivers copy your breathing, moving, and chanting.

Stretch and Bounce

MUSIC CONTENT

Usual Duple Meter

MOVEMENT CONTENT

FLOW
Continuous Flow
Continuous Flow with Pulsations
Same and Different

MATERIALS NEEDED

Space for free movement

Parachute

Moderate   Edwin E. Gordon

ACCULTURATION

Perform the chant using neutral syllables. Demonstrate continuous flow with your upper body using your torso, shoulders, and arms to stretch and bounce as you perform each two-measure rhythm pattern of the chant. Follow this activity with Acculturation Patterns and Activities suggested on the facing page.

IMITATION

(1) Perform the chant as in the Acculturation Activity. When performing measures 3, 4, 7, 8, 11, and 12, do not perform the chant out loud. Audiate and move during those measures. (2) Perform the chant as described in the previous Imitation Activity while having each child and caregiver hold the edge of a parachute. (3) Perform the chant as in the Acculturation Activity. After the last macrobeat of the chant, add a long *Shhh!* and accompany yourself with continuous movement. Involve the whole body, as if you are a balloon that is losing air. Follow each activity with Imitation Patterns and Activities suggested on the facing page.

ASSIMILATION

Perform the chant as in the Acculturation Activity. Add pulsations to each microbeat. Encourage the children to imitate your movements. Then, perform the chant and move continuously without pulsations, and encourage the children to move like you. Ask the children if your two performances were the same or different. Have the children discuss their answers. After the children decide that the performances were different, tell them that in the first performance it was as if they were giving their body parts smooth rides. In the second performance, it was as if they were giving themselves bumpy rides. Perform the chant again. Tell the children to choose to give smooth rides or bumpy rides. Provide more opportunities to coordinate moving using continuous flow with pulsations. Follow this activity with Assimilation Patterns and Activities suggested on the facing page.

ACCULTURATION

STAGE 1:   Child is building a listening vocabulary by hearing music and watching and feeling continuous movement.

STAGE 2:   Child responds with sound or movement babble that is not specifically related to the activity.

STAGE 3:   Child responds with related sound or movement babble during the activity or immediately after a repetition of the activity.

Acculturation Pattern Activity:

After the last repetition of the chant, perform Acculturation Patterns. Continuously move your shoulders, back, and hips during each pattern. Sometimes move quickly, and sometimes move slowly during each pattern. Do not vary the tempo of the patterns.

IMITATION AND ASSIMILATION PATTERNS / RHYTHM

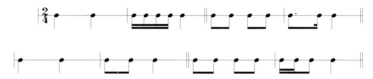

IMITATION

STAGE 4:   Child becomes aware that his responses are different from the adult's music and movement model.

STAGE 5:   Child responds with more precise imitation of rhythm patterns and movements.

Imitation Pattern Activity:

Continuously move your shoulders, back, and hips as you breathe and perform each pattern. Sometimes move quickly, and sometimes move slowly during each pattern. Do not vary the tempo of the patterns. Imitate a child's inaccurate response and non-verbally encourage a chanting dialogue with him using his inaccurate pattern. Continue chanting Imitation and Assimilation Patterns for the child until he performs an audiation stare, at which time, he should be phased into Stage 5. For children who are in Stage 5, the adult imitates the rhythm pattern responses made by the child, then performs two sets of microbeats in Usual Duple meter, repeats the original rhythm pattern and non-verbally encourages the child to imitate it.

ASSIMILATION

STAGE 6:   Child develops an awareness of his lack of coordination between his breathing and moving, and breathing and chanting by continuously moving and pulsating microbeats as the teacher chants BAH to macrobeats. Then, while performing the same type of movement, the child imitates the rhythm patterns chanted by the teacher.

STAGE 7:   Child coordinates his breathing, moving, and chanting while imitating rhythm patterns precisely.

Assimilation Pattern Activity:

After the last repetition of the chant, perform Assimilation Patterns. Before each pattern, breathe as you bend your knees. Swing your arms from back to front, and jump, landing on the first macrobeat of each pattern. Continuously move your shoulders, back, and hips as you chant each pattern. Sometimes move quickly, and sometimes move slowly during each pattern. Encourage the children to repeat after you and to imitate your movements.

Walking with My Mom

MUSIC CONTENT

Usual Duple Meter

Accent

MOVEMENT CONTENT

FLOW
Continuous Flow

WEIGHT
Strong, Gentle

SPACE
Locomotor
Pathways

COORDINATED BREATHING
Audiating, Moving, Chanting

MATERIALS NEEDED

Space for free movement

One tennis ball per person

Bubble liquid and wand

Moderate   Edwin E. Gordon

ACCULTURATION

Chant *Walking With My Mom* using a moderate tempo. Be certain to observe the accent marks in the last two measures. Ask caregivers to place infants who are awake on their backs and invite their caregivers to gently move the babies' feet in a peddling motion. Repeat the chant, next time moving infants' hands. Finally, stand holding an infant and move with flow while you chant. (With toddlers and older children, model continuous flow in self space as you chant.) Invite the adults to chant with you when they know the chant. Follow these movements with Acculturation Patterns and Activities suggested on the facing page.

IMITATION

(1) Sit knee-to-knee or foot-to-foot in a circle. Perform the chant while modeling continuous flow in your upper body. When you chant the last measure, move your hands bilaterally away from you with strong flow (as if you were rolling a ball away). (2) After children begin to imitate you, place the whole bag of balls in front of you. Place one ball in each hand and repeat the continuous flowing movements described in Imitation Activity (1). At the end of the chant, roll the balls to children in the circle using strong flow. Invite the children who receive balls to roll them away at the same time you do at the end of the chant. Follow these activities with Imitation Patterns and Activities suggested on the facing page.

ASSIMILATION

Model walking in self space to microbeats using random pathways as you chant. Invite children to move as you were moving. Then, perform the duet while holding hands with an adult, continuing to walk to microbeats in random pathways. Tell the children that when they hear both adults chanting the same music, they are to walk to microbeats in self space. When they hear adults chanting different music at the same time (duet), they are to walk to microbeats in shared space. Follow these activities with Assimilation Patterns and Activities suggested on the facing page.

WALKING WITH MY MOM DUET

ACCULTURATION PATTERNS / RHYTHM

ACCULTURATION

STAGE 1:   Child is building a listening vocabulary by hearing music and watching and feeling continuous movement.

STAGE 2:   Child responds with sound or movement babble that is not specifically related to the activity.

STAGE 3:   Child responds with related sound or movement babble during the activity or immediately after a repetition of the activity.

Acculturation Pattern Activity:

Chant Acculturation Patterns, and invite adults to be your echo. Then, ask adults not to echo, and provide individual children an opportunity to hear only your patterns and silence. Make eye contact with each child as you chant and listen.

IMITATION AND ASSIMILATION PATTERNS / RHYTHM

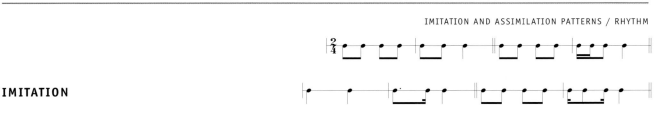

IMITATION

STAGE 4:   Child becomes aware that his responses are different from the adult's music and movement model.

STAGE 5:   Child responds with more precise imitation of rhythm patterns and movements.

Imitation Pattern Activity:

Take a breath and chant an Imitation and Assimilation Pattern. Roll a ball to the child on the first macrobeat of the pattern. Imitate a child's inaccurate response and non-verbally encourage a chanting dialogue with him using his inaccurate pattern. Continue chanting Imitation and Assimilation Patterns for the child until he performs an audiation stare, at which time, he should be phased into Stage 5. For children who are in Stage 5, the adult imitates the rhythm pattern responses made by the child, then performs two sets of microbeats in Usual Duple meter, repeats the original rhythm pattern and non-verbally encourages the child to imitate it.

ASSIMILATION

STAGE 6:   Child develops an awareness of his lack of coordination between his breathing and moving, and breathing and chanting by continuously moving and pulsating microbeats as the teacher chants BAH to macrobeats. Then, while performing the same type of movement, the child imitates the inaccurate rhythm patterns chanted by the teacher.

STAGE 7:   Child coordinates his breathing, moving, and chanting while imitating rhythm patterns precisely.

Assimilation Pattern Activity:

Model a full macrobeat breath and chant an Imitation and Assimilation Pattern. Model a breath again, and blow a steady gentle stream of air while you audiate a four-macrobeat pattern. Ask the child to breathe and blow gently with you for the length of four macrobeats. Repeat the sequence, blowing bubbles from the wand. Finally, ask the child to breathe and blow bubbles at the same time you breathe and chant a four-macrobeat pattern.

Fireworks

Moderate   Edwin E. Gordon

Shoo!

ACCULTURATION

Perform the chant while modeling continuous flow. Alternate slow continuous flow with quick continuous flow every two measures. Be certain to include a *crescendo* as you sustain the first two measures. In measure 5, perform the short rhythm pattern *subito piano* (suddenly quietly). Perform measure 8 *subito forte* (suddenly loudly). Clap your hands or pat the floor during the macrobeat rest at the end of the chant. Follow this activity with Acculturation Patterns and Activities suggested on the facing page.

IMITATION

(1) Repeat the Acculturation Activity and encourage children to imitate your movements. (2) Choreograph the chant. Begin standing in self space, using a lot of space as you flow, pulsate, and hop. Measures 1 and 2: Model slow flow. Measures 3 and 4: Model quick flow. Measures 5 and 6: Pulsate macrobeats. Measures 7 and first half of measure 8: Pat your legs and prepare to hop. Second macrobeat: Hop with a clap so you land to the last macrobeat of measure 8. Follow this activity with Imitation Patterns and Activities suggested on the facing page.

ASSIMILATION

(1) After children are familiar with the previous Acculturation and Imitation Activities, invite them to move their whole bodies with continuous flow. In the silence, audiate *Fireworks* in the tempo children would expect you to perform it. Begin pulsating microbeats in that tempo and ask children to move like you. Finally, as you continue moving, ask children to chant TAH to microbeats. Assist them in beginning, but do not chant with them. (2) After children are able to chant microbeats, tell them you will chant *Fireworks*. When they hear you chanting, they should pulsate and silently audiate TAH to microbeats. When you finish chanting, they should continue to pulsate and chant microbeats out loud. Follow this activity with Assimilation Patterns and Activities suggested on the facing page.

ACCULTURATION PATTERNS / RHYTHM

ACCULTURATION

STAGE 1: Child is building a listening vocabulary by hearing music and watching and feeling continuous movement.

STAGE 2: Child responds with sound or movement babble that is not specifically related to the activity.

STAGE 3: Child responds with related sound or movement babble during the activity or immediately after a repetition of the activity.

Acculturation Pattern Activity:

After a few repetitions of the chant, pause briefly. Then chant patterns for individual children. Invite all adults to move with continuous flow while you are with individual children.

IMITATION AND ASSIMILATION PATTERNS / RHYTHM

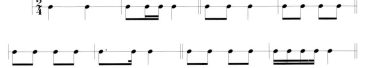

IMITATION

STAGE 4: Child becomes aware that his responses are different from the adult's music and movement model.

STAGE 5: Child responds with more precise imitation of rhythm patterns and movements.

Imitation Pattern Activity:

When performing the chant, silently audiate measures 7 and 8, but continue to perform movements suggested in the Imitation Activity. Then, perform Imitation Patterns for children. If a child's response disrupts the tempo or meter you are chanting, imitate his response, and then perform a repetition of *Fireworks* in the original tempo. Then resume pattern instruction. Imitate a child's inaccurate response and non-verbally encourage a chanting dialogue with him using his inaccurate pattern. Continue chanting Imitation and Assimilation Patterns for the child until he performs an audiation stare, at which time, he should be phased into Stage 5. For children who are in Stage 5, the adult imitates the inaccurate rhythm pattern responses made by the child, then performs two sets of microbeats in Usual Duple meter, repeats the original rhythm pattern and non-verbally encourages the child to imitate it.

ASSIMILATION

STAGE 6: Child develops an awareness of his lack of coordination between his breathing and moving, and breathing and chanting by continuously moving and pulsating microbeats as the teacher chants BAH to macrobeats. Then, while performing the same type of movement, the child imitates the rhythm patterns chanted by the teacher.

STAGE 7: Child coordinates his breathing, moving and chanting while imitating rhythm patterns precisely.

Assimilation Pattern Activity:

Ask children to be your echo. Chant an Imitation and Assimilation Pattern and gesture for them to breathe before they chant it together. When they are successful coordinating their breathing and chanting, ask them to silently audiate your chant as they move like you. Tell them they will finish the chant with the pattern they just performed. Model movements from Imitation or Assimilation Activities on the previous page while you chant *Fireworks*. Gesture for them to breathe before they chant the pattern. Ask children whether the pattern they performed was the same as or different from the pattern they are used to hearing at the end of *Fireworks*. Do not explain why, but do tell them if the pattern was the same or different.

Rolling

MUSIC CONTENT

Usual Triple Meter

MOVEMENT CONTENT

FLOW
Continuous Flow

COORDINATED BREATHING
Audiating, Moving, Chanting

MATERIALS NEEDED

Space for free movement

Two tennis balls per person

Moderate   Wendy H. Valerio

ACCULTURATION

   Perform the chant using neutral syllables. Hold a child as you continuously move around the room, or let children watch you continuously move around the room. Emphasize continuous movement by drawing imaginary circles with your shoulders, back, and hips as you travel. Follow this activity with Acculturation Patterns and Activities suggested on the facing page.

IMITATION

   (1) Encourage children to "sit upon their sit-upons" during this entire activity. Have the children sit on the floor in a circle, knee-to-knee or foot-to-foot. Give each child 2 tennis balls, one for each hand. Perform the chant using neutral syllables. Continuously rock and sway as you chant. Encourage the children to move like you, giving each tennis ball a ride. Roll the balls across the circle on the first macrobeat of the fourth measure. (2) Perform the chant as in the previous Imitation Activity; however, audiate and move measures 1, 2, and 3. Perform measure 4 out loud as you roll the balls across the circle. Encourage children to imitate your movements. Follow each activity with Imitation Patterns and Activities suggested on the facing page.

ASSIMILATION

   (1) Perform the chant as in Imitation Activity 1; however, demonstrate continuous movements with pulsations to microbeats. Emphasize movement of your shoulders, back, and hips. (2) Perform the chant several times as in the first Imitation Activity described above. Then, audiate and move measures 1, 2, 3, and perform measure 4 out loud as you roll the balls across the circle. Encourage children to imitate your movements. Follow each activity with Assimilation Patterns and Activities suggested on the facing page.

ACCULTURATION PATTERNS / RHYTHM

ACCULTURATION

STAGE 1: Child is building a listening vocabulary by hearing music and watching and feeling continuous movement.

STAGE 2: Child responds with sound or movement babble that is not specifically related to the activity.

STAGE 3: Child responds with related sound or movement babble during the activity or immediately after a repetition of the activity.

Acculturation Pattern Activity

After several repetitions of the chant perform Acculturation Patterns. Hold a child and move him continuously as you chant each pattern. Have other caregivers hold a child, move continuously, and repeat after you.

IMITATION AND ASSIMILATION PATTERNS / RHYTHM

IMITATION

STAGE 4: Child becomes aware that his responses are different from the adult's music and movement model.

STAGE 5: Child responds with more precise imitation of rhythm patterns and movements.

Imitation Pattern Activity:

Give a ball a ride as you chant a pattern. Roll the ball to a child, releasing the ball on the third macrobeat of each pattern. Repeat the process for each child. Encourage children to catch the ball and roll it back to you. If a child responds with an inaccurate pattern, imitate his inaccurate response and non-verbally encourage a pattern dialogue with the child. Continue chanting Imitation and Assimilation Patterns for the child until he performs an audiation stare, at which time, he should be phased into Stage 5. For children who are in Stage 5, the adult imitates the inaccurate rhythm pattern responses made by the child, then performs two sets of microbeats in Usual Triple meter in the original tempo that patterns were presented, repeats the original rhythm pattern, and encourages the child to imitate it.

ASSIMILATION

STAGE 6: Child develops an awareness of his lack of coordination between his breathing and moving, and breathing and chanting by continuously moving and pulsating microbeats as the teacher chants BAH to macrobeats. Then, while performing the same type of movement, the child imitates the rhythm patterns chanted by the teacher.

STAGE 7: Child coordinates his breathing, moving, and chanting while imitating rhythm patterns precisely.

Assimilation Pattern Activity

Pretend to give a ball a ride as you chant a pattern. Take a deep, relaxing breath before each pattern you chant and move. Roll the ball to a child, releasing the ball on the third macrobeat of each pattern. Repeat the process for each child. Encourage children to catch the ball, give it a ride and roll it back to you. Ask the children to tell you what you do before you chant and move each pattern (breathe).

Popsicle

Edwin E. Gordon

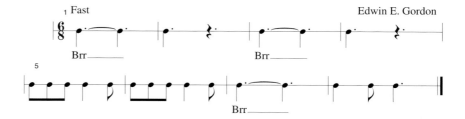

Brr____ Brr____ Brr____

MUSIC CONTENT

Usual Triple Meter

Dynamics: Crescendo, Decrescendo

Same and Different

MOVEMENT CONTENT

FLOW
Continuous Flow

TIME
Quick, Slow

COORDINATED BREATHING
Audiating, Moving, Chanting
Same and Different

MATERIALS NEEDED

Space for free movement

Tambourine

ACCULTURATION

(1) Perform the chant using neutral syllables, substituting a rapid tongue roll for each *Brr.* Perform the chant once while modeling slow continuous flow and, without changing the tempo of the chant, perform it once modeling quick flow. (2) For each *Brr,* tickle a child. On the first macrobeat of measures 2 and 4, end the tickle by hugging the child. In measures 5 and 6, crawl your fingers up the child's tummy until the next *Brr,* during which you return to the tickling followed by a hug. Follow this activity with Acculturation Patterns and Activities suggested on the facing page.

IMITATION

(1) During the sustained *Brrs* in the chant, model slow continuous flow while rapidly shaking a tambourine. Freeze during the rests. During measures 5 and 6, play the tambourine to macrobeats, resuming the shake and moving with continuous flow in measure 7. Play the last rhythm pattern in measure 8 on the tambourine as you chant it. (2) Show children how to shake the tambourine, and invite a child to be the leader. When he shakes the tambourine, everyone should move with continuous flow. When the tambourine is silent, everyone should freeze. Do not perform the chant when a child is playing the tambourine. Follow each activity with Imitation Patterns and Activities suggested on the facing page.

ASSIMILATION

(1) Perform the four-macrobeat pattern of the chant notated in measures 5 and 6, and gesture for individual children to imitate you. Be certain to model a breath before you begin. Tell children you will gesture for individuals to perform that rhythm pattern during *Popsicle.* Perform the chant as notated, and gesture for individual children to breathe and chant the pattern when it occurs in the chant. Model and ask children to move with continuous flow throughout. (2) Ask children to audiate four-macrobeat patterns that are different from the one that they chanted in the previous activity. Tell them you will begin *Popsicle* as usual, but when you gesture for individuals to chant, ask them to chant a different rhythm pattern. Follow each activity with Assimilation Patterns and Activities suggested on the facing page.

ACCULTURATION

STAGE 1:   Child is building a listening vocabulary by hearing music and watching and feeling continuous movement.

STAGE 2:   Child responds with sound or movement babble that is not specifically related to the activity.

STAGE 3:   Child responds with related sound or movement babble during the activity or immediately after a repetition of the activity.

Acculturation Pattern Activity:

After the last repetition of the chant, pause briefly. Then perform the patterns for individual children in the same tempo you have been performing *Popsicle*. Move with continuous flow while you chant patterns.

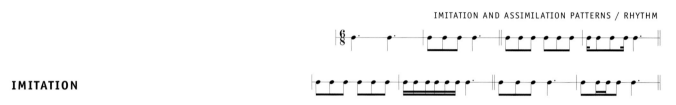

IMITATION

STAGE 4:   Child becomes aware that his responses are different from the adult's music and movement model.

STAGE 5:   Child responds with more precise imitation of rhythm patterns and movements.

Imitation Pattern Activity

Intersperse pattern instruction between repetitions of the chant. If a child inaccurately imitates a rhythm pattern, imitate his inaccurate response and non-verbally encourage a pattern dialogue with him. Continue chanting Imitation and Assimilation Patterns for the child until he performs an audiation stare, at which time, he should be phased into Stage 5. For children who are in Stage 5, the adult imitates the inaccurate rhythm pattern responses made by the child, then performs two sets of microbeats in Usual Triple meter in the original tempo that patterns were presented, repeats the original rhythm pattern, and non-verbally encourages the child to imitate it.

ASSIMILATION

STAGE 6:   Child develops an awareness of his lack of coordination between his breathing and moving, and breathing and chanting by continuously moving and pulsating microbeats as the teacher chants BAH to macrobeats. Then, while performing the same type of movement, the child imitates the rhythm patterns chanted by the teacher.

STAGE 7:   Child coordinates his breathing, moving, and chanting while imitating rhythm patterns precisely.

Assimilation Pattern Activity

Audiate *Popsicle* silently in the tempo children would expect you to perform it. Model continuous flow and ask children to move like you. Ask them to observe your movement, for you will be changing it and you want them to change with you. When children are moving with flow, change your movements to pulsating microbeats with continuous flow. Allow children to change their movements and then invite them to chant TAH to each microbeat. Assist them in beginning, but do not continue to chant with them. Instead, chant BAH to each macrobeat while you pulsate to microbeats. Finally, tell the children to chant and pulsate microbeats while you chant *Popsicle*.

Child Song

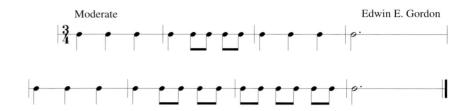

Moderate   Edwin E. Gordon

MUSIC CONTENT

Usual Triple Meter

MOVEMENT CONTENT

SPACE
Stationary

COORDINATED BREATHING
Audiating, Moving, Chanting

MATERIALS NEEDED

Finger cymbals

Triangle and striker

Egg shakers

ACCULTURATION

Perform the chant using neutral syllables as you stand in self space and rock from side-to-side, or while in shared space as you hold an infant or young child. At the end of the chant, cease all of your movement and remain very quiet. Then repeat chanting and rocking. If you are in self space, substitute rocking with swinging or pushing and pulling movements. Two adults can hold the hands and feet of a toddler or older child who enjoys being swung, and swing him from side-to-side to the macrobeats of the chant. Follow this activity with Acculturation Patterns and Activities suggested on the facing page.

IMITATION

Hold one finger cymbal stationary and parallel to the floor and strike it with another finger cymbal as you chant. Invite adults and children to continue rocking, swinging, or pushing and pulling. Encourage children to move like the adults. Give children an opportunity to imitate your playing. Play triangle and shakers to macrobeats for children to imitate. Do not tell them to play to the macrobeats and do not expect them to do so. Instead, either model the macrobeats on your lap or gently tap children's shoulders from behind them while they play. Follow this activity with Imitation Patterns and Activities suggested on the facing page.

ASSIMILATION

Have finger cymbals, triangles, and shakers available for children to share. Repeat the Acculturation and Imitation Activities above for review. Tell the children that if they hear *Child Song*, they are to play their instruments, but if they hear different music, they are to listen. (Intersperse chants in meters different from *Child Song*, such as *Stretch and Bounce*, or songs such as *Winter Day* and allow the children to listen and play.) Follow this activity with Assimilation Patterns and Activities suggested on the facing page.

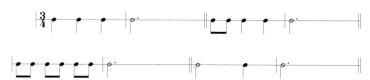

ACCULTURATION

STAGE 1: Child is building a listening vocabulary by hearing music and watching and feeling continuous movement.
STAGE 2: Child responds with sound or movement babble that is not specifically related to the activity.
STAGE 3: Child responds with related sound or movement babble during the activity or immediately after a repetition of the activity.

Acculturation Pattern Activity

After the last repetition of the chant, perform patterns for individual children. Explore different sound effects with your voice as you perform.

IMITATION AND ASSIMILATION PATTERNS / RHYTHM

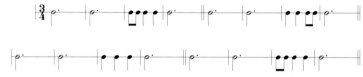

IMITATION

STAGE 4: Child becomes aware that his responses are different from the adult's music and movement model.
STAGE 5: Child responds with more precise imitation of rhythm patterns and movements.

Imitation Pattern Activity

Intersperse Imitation Patterns between repetitions of the chant for children who are ready for them. Imitate a child's inaccurate response and non-verbally encourage a chanting dialogue with him using his inaccurate pattern. Continue chanting Imitation and Assimilation Patterns for the child until he performs an audiation stare, at which time, he should be phased into Stage 5. For children who are in Stage 5, the adult imitates the rhythm pattern responses made by the child, then performs two sets of microbeats in Usual Triple meter in the original tempo that patterns were presented, repeats the original rhythm pattern, and non-verbally encourages the child to imitate it. At the end of the activity, you can request that each child with an instrument vocally echo your pattern prior to giving the instrument back to you.

ASSIMILATION

STAGE 6: Child develops an awareness of his lack of coordination between his breathing and moving, and breathing and chanting by continuously moving and pulsating microbeats as the teacher chants BAH on macrobeats. Then, while performing the same type of movement, the child imitates the rhythm patterns chanted by the teacher.
STAGE 7: Child coordinates his breathing, moving, and chanting while imitating rhythm patterns precisely.

Assimilation Pattern Activity

Give egg shakers to children, one for each hand. Show them how to flow so the egg shakers do not make a sound. Then, show them how to pulsate to the microbeats of the chant so the egg shakers will make a sound. Perform the chant, and model pulsating movements to the microbeats. At the end of the chant, continue to pulsate, inviting the children to chant TAH to each microbeat. Once they are moving and chanting, begin chanting BAH to macrobeats as you pulsate microbeats. Be certain not to chant TAH with the children.

Snowflake

Edwin E. Gordon

Moderate

MUSIC CONTENT

Harmonic Minor Tonality

Usual Triple Meter

MOVEMENT CONTENT

FLOW
Continuous Flow

TIME
Quick, Slow

SPACE
Open, Closed Shapes
Same and Different

MATERIALS NEEDED

Space for free movement

ACCULTURATION

(1) Stand and perform the chant using neutral syllables. When you are making sounds during measures 1, 2, 5, and 6 move quickly by flicking your arms and hands. Freeze during the silences in those measures. During measures 3 and 4 roll your arms. During measures 7 and 8 twirl to the ground. (2) For a variation perform as above and use the neutral syllables *Uh-oh* in measures 1, 2, 5, and 6. Follow each activity with Acculturation Patterns and Activities suggested on the facing page.

IMITATION

Perform the chant and movements as in the previous Acculturation Activity. After the children are familiar with the chant and movements, audiate the chant silently while performing the movements. Begin your audiation and movement with the following preparatory phrase in the meter and tempo of the chant. Follow this activity with Imitation Patterns and Activities suggested on the facing page.

Bum, bum, bum, rea-dy chant.

ASSIMILATION

Perform the chant and movements as in the previous Acculturation and Imitation Activities. After the children are familiar with the activities, ask them to make interesting body shapes after each twirl at the end of the chant. Sometimes instruct them to make shapes that make spaces. Sometimes instruct them to make shapes that do not make spaces. Sometimes ask the children to compare the shapes they have made. Ask them, "What makes these two shapes the same?", or "What makes these two shapes different?" Follow this activity with Assimilation Patterns and Activities suggested on the facing page.

ACCULTURATION

STAGE 1: Child is building a listening vocabulary by hearing music and watching and feeling continuous movement.

STAGE 2: Child responds with sound or movement babble that is not specifically related to the activity.

STAGE 3: Child responds with related sound or movement babble during the activity or immediately after a repetition of the activity.

Acculturation Pattern Activity

Chant each pattern and have caregivers repeat after you. Sometimes sound strong, and sometimes sound gentle. Breathe and then move continuously as you chant each pattern. Make eye contact with individual children during each pattern you chant.

IMITATION AND ASSIMILATION PATTERNS / RHYTHM

IMITATION

STAGE 4: Child becomes aware that his responses are different from the adult's music and movement model.

STAGE 5: Child responds with more precise imitation of rhythm patterns and movements.

Imitation Pattern Activity:

Chant each pattern and have caregivers and children repeat after you. Breathe before you chant and move continuously as you chant each pattern. Imitate a child's inaccurate response and non-verbally encourage a chanting dialogue with him using his inaccurate pattern. Continue chanting Imitation and Assimilation Patterns for the child until he performs an audiation stare, at which time, he should be phased into Stage 5. For children who are in Stage 5, the adult imitates the inaccurate rhythm pattern responses made by the child, then performs two sets of microbeats in Usual Triple meter in the original tempo that patterns were presented, repeats the original rhythm pattern, and non-verbally encourages the child to imitate it.

ASSIMILATION

STAGE 6: Child develops an awareness of his lack of coordination between his breathing and moving, and breathing and chanting by continuously moving and pulsating microbeats as the teacher chants BAH to macrobeats. Then, while performing the same type of movement, the child imitates the rhythm patterns chanted by the teacher.

STAGE 7: Child coordinates his breathing, moving, and chanting while imitating rhythm patterns precisely.

Assimilation Pattern Activity:

Tell the children you are going to perform two rhythm patterns for them. The patterns may sound the same, or they may sound different. If the patterns sound the same the children should hold up hands that look the same. If the patterns sound different, the children should hold up hands that look different. Play the game several times to help the children begin to notice the sameness and difference between rhythm patterns.

Rain

MUSIC CONTENT

Unusual Paired Meter

Timbre Awareness

MOVEMENT CONTENT

FLOW
Continuous Flow
Continuous Flow with Pulsations

SPACE
Stationary

COORDINATED BREATHING
Audiating, Moving, Chanting

MATERIALS NEEDED

Space for free movement

Rain stick

Moderate   Edwin E. Gordon

ACCULTURATION

(1) Perform the chant using neutral syllables while modeling continuous, fluid movement in your shoulders, hips, and back. After several repetitions, cease movement and chanting. Pause until children interrupt the silence, then resume chanting and moving. (2) After a repetition of the chant, lower one end of a rain stick to produce an even, gentle rain sound. Ask children to move as in the first Acculturation Activity when they hear the rain sound, but to freeze if they hear the chant. Allow children to explore making sounds with the rain stick.

IMITATION

(1) Perform the chant as you did for the Acculturation Activity, this time encouraging children to imitate your movements. (2) Model continuous movements, such as twisting, bending, pushing, pulling, or rocking to macrobeats in self or shared space. Encourage children to imitate your movements.

ASSIMILATION

(1) Model continuous flow with pulsations to microbeats in the tempo children would expect you to perform *Rain*. Chant TAH to each microbeat as you move. Invite the children to chant TAH as they move continuously with pulsations. As soon as they begin chanting, be certain not to chant with them. Model microbeat pulsations for them as you chant BAH to each macrobeat. (2) Ask children to pulsate microbeats with continuous flow while chanting TAH to each microbeat. When they have begun chanting microbeats, accompany them by chanting *Rain*.

Panda

Moderate   Edwin E. Gordon

ACCULTURATION

Perform the chant using neutral syllables. Twist from side-to-side as you chant. Sometimes allow the children to observe you, and sometimes hold a child as you twist and chant.

IMITATION

(1) While seated, perform the chant using neutral syllables as you continuously rock from side-to-side. Perform the chant again and rock from front to back. Then, ask children to stand behind caregivers and to gently rock the caregivers from front to back by holding on to their shoulders. (2) Give each child a hula hoop. Have each child sit inside the hoop, hold it with each hand and rock from side-to-side as you perform the chant.

ASSIMILATION

Have each caregiver face one or two children while seated on the floor. Give each child one rhythm stick. Have each child and caregiver hold the stick horizontally and pull back and forth in a rowing motion to macrobeats as you perform the chant. If one caregiver is working with two children, the caregiver may hold a rhythm stick in each hand, one for each child. After the children are familiar with this activity, have them chant TAH to microbeats as they row and as you perform the chant.

MUSIC CONTENT

Unusual Paired Meter

MOVEMENT CONTENT

FLOW
Continuous Flow
Continuous Flow with Pulsations

SPACE
Stationary

COORDINATED BREATHING
Audiating, Moving, Chanting

MATERIALS NEEDED

Space for free movement
One rhythm stick for each child
One hula hoop for each child

Buggy Ride

MUSIC CONTENT

Unusual Unpaired Meter

Accent

MOVEMENT CONTENT

FLOW
Continuous Flow
Continuous Flow with Pulsations

SPACE
Pathways

COORDINATED BREATHING
Audiating, Moving, Chanting

MATERIALS NEEDED

Space for free movement

Fast   Wendy H. Valerio

ACCULTURATION

Perform the chant using neutral syllables. While seated, demonstrate continuous flow with your upper body using your torso, shoulders, arms, and hips to sway and rock to macrobeats. Make eye contact with individual children as you perform. Repeat several times.

IMITATION

(1) Perform the chant using neutral syllables while demonstrating continuous flow with your upper body using your torso, shoulders, arms, and hips to sway and rock to macrobeats. Pat the floor simultaneously with both hands (bilateral movement) as you perform the last three macrobeats of the chant. Stretch your arms wide on the final macrobeat to demonstrate its length. (2) Perform the chant while demonstrating the movements described in the previous Imitation Activity. When performing the final measure do not chant out loud. Rather, audiate and bilaterally pat the floor with both hands. To reinforce continuous flow, never pat in the same place twice.

ASSIMILATION

(1) Perform the chant using neutral syllables while demonstrating continuous movement as in the Acculturation and Imitation Activities. Have pairs of children or pairs of children and caregivers bilaterally hold hands and move continuously as you chant. You may tell them to draw imaginary circles in space while holding hands. (2) Perform the chant while demonstrating continuous movement as in the Acculturation and Imitation Activities. Have pairs of children or pairs of children and caregivers bilaterally hold hands and move continuously and pulse macrobeats as you chant. (3) Perform the chant while demonstrating continuous movement as in the Acculturation and Imitation Activities. Have pairs of children or pairs of children and caregivers bilaterally hold hands and move continuously and pulse macrobeats while chanting TAH to each microbeat as you perform BAH to each macrobeat. Then have the children continue moving and chanting as you perform *Buggy Ride.*

Wild Pony

Moderate   Edwin E. Gordon

MUSIC CONTENT

Unusual Unpaired Meter

Accent

MOVEMENT CONTENT

BODY AWARENESS
Body Parts

FLOW
Continuous Flow

FLOW
Continuous Flow with Pulsations

SPACE
Stationary

MATERIALS NEEDED

Space for free movement

ACCULTURATION

(1) Perform the chant with accents as written while modeling continuous flow. After a few repetitions of the chant, add pressing movements to the accents. Press, making large gestures with your hands, elbows, knees, and hips. (2) Place an infant or toddler on your lap and hold the child's hands. Perform the chant and bounce the child to the macrobeats.

IMITATION

Perform the chant as described in Acculturation Activity (1). Encourage children to imitate your movements. After they have imitated continuous flow, invite them to suggest body parts to press to the accented macrobeats. Do not expect them to move accurately to macrobeats. If children move in ways different from you, imitate their movements.

ASSIMILATION

(1) Pair each child with an adult or another child and have the two face each other. Perform the chant with accents, and model pats in different places to the microbeats. After several repetitions of the chant, invite pairs to sit one behind the other. Have the person in back pat microbeats in different places on the back and shoulders of his partner. (2) Sit in self space. Model patting in different places while chanting microbeats using TAH. Invite the children to join you. As soon as the children begin to chant, you begin chanting BAH to macrobeats as you move.

Train Ride

Edwin E. Gordon

MUSIC CONTENT

Unusual Unpaired Meter

Accent

MOVEMENT CONTENT

FLOW
Continuous Flow
Continuous Flow with Pulsations

SPACE
Locomotor

COORDINATED BREATHING
Audiating, Moving, Chanting

MATERIALS NEEDED

Space for free movement

Moderate

ACCULTURATION

(1) Perform *Train Ride* with suggested accents while modeling continuous flow. Ask caregivers to listen and to model movements like yours. When caregivers know the chant, ask them to chant while they move. (2) Place a very young child on your knees or in your lap. Bounce him on small bounces to microbeats as you chant, exaggerating the bounces as you perform accents.

IMITATION

Invite the children to board your train. Form a long walking line as you sing *Down by the Station* (*Music Play*, p. 100). When everyone is on board the train and your song is finished, ask the children where the train should go (to the zoo, park, gardens, or beach). Tell them they are on the FLOW TRAIN to their destination. They should follow you and move with continuous flow to stay on the train. Chant *Train Ride* and model slow continuous flow as you perform the chant with suggested accents. When you have repeated the chant several times and have led the train with locomotor flow, apply the strong brakes as you make a *Chhh* sound. Pantomime movements to compliment the destination chosen by the children. Perform other melodies from *Music Play* while you are pantomiming movements. Then, board the FLOW TRAIN and return back to music class while performing *Down By the Station*.

ASSIMILATION

Invite the children to be the fuel that makes the train move. Some trains need coal and steam, others need electricity. Your train needs microbeats. Model continuous pulsating flow while chanting TAH to the microbeat pattern notated below. Ask children to move and chant like you. As soon as they chant microbeats, begin chanting BAH to macrobeats as notated in the second pattern below. Be certain children do not begin chanting macrobeats, too. Ask individual children if they would be your fuel as the rest of the children are the FLOW TRAIN behind you and the fuel. Take turns as children agree to try chanting microbeats and moving individually.

Microbeat Pattern   Macrobeat Pattern

songs with words

Down by the Station

MUSIC CONTENT

Major Tonality

Usual Duple Meter

MOVEMENT CONTENT

WEIGHT
Strong, Gentle

SPACE
Stationary, Locomotor

COORDINATED BREATHING
Audiating, Moving, Chanting

MATERIALS NEEDED

Space for free movement

Train whistle, optional

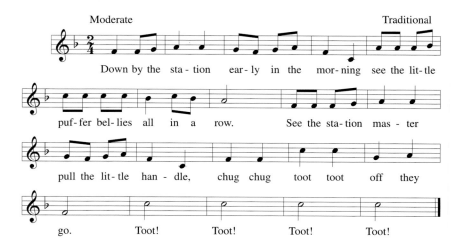

Moderate   Traditional

Down by the sta-tion ear-ly in the mor-ning see the lit-tle

puf-fer bel-lies all in a row.   See the sta-tion mas-ter

pull the lit-tle han-dle, chug chug toot toot off they

go.   Toot!   Toot!   Toot!   Toot!

ACCULTURATION

Form a seated train alternating adults and children, with a child at the front of the train. Have each person in the train place their hands on the backs of the person in front of them. Join the train and rock forward and back to macrobeats as you sing. (With toddlers who are walking, each caregiver and child can make two-person chariots. The caregiver stands in front of the child, both facing forward and each holding both hands. The chariots can walk together to the macrobeats as just described.)

IMITATION

Invite everyone to walk to microbeats as you sing *Down by the Station*. Ask caregivers to make strong *Chhh* train sounds on the macrobeats as they walk to microbeats and you sing the melody. Remind caregivers to take breaths as needed! In between repetitions of the song, improvise four-macrobeat patterns in Usual Duple meter using the *Chhh* sound, and invite everyone to be your echo. Sometimes make strong *Chhh* sounds, and other times make gentle *Chhh* sounds. End the activity by blowing a long sound on a train whistle.

ASSIMILATION

Children who are able to imitate patterns from the Imitation Activity above should be encouraged to take full macrobeat breaths prior to echoing your patterns. Model a full macrobeat breath in the tempo you have been performing *Down by the Station* and exhale on a *Chhh* sound for four macrobeats while modeling continuous flow. Gesture for children to breathe and then echo you and your flow. Repeat, this time chanting four-macrobeat rhythm patterns for children to echo while moving with continuous flow.

Jeremiah Blow the Fire

MUSIC CONTENT
Major Tonality
Usual Duple Meter

MOVEMENT CONTENT
FLOW
Continuous Flow
COORDINATED BREATHING
Audiating, Moving, Singing

MATERIALS NEEDED
Space for free movement
One chiffon scarf per person

ACCULTURATION

Have each caregiver place a chiffon scarf over her head. Perform the song with text as you sway. Have each caregiver copy your singing and moving and make eye contact with individual children. After completing the song, take a big breath and blow the scarf to a child. Repeat several times, then put a scarf on each child's head. After completing the song as you continuously sway, take a big breath and demonstrate how to blow as you gently pull the scarf off of each child's head.

IMITATION

Give each child and caregiver a scarf and perform the song as in the previous Acculturation Activity. When children and caregivers are familiar with the song and activity, quietly instruct the caregivers to audiate, but not to sing the phrase *puff, puff, puff*. Perform the song as in previous repetitions and listen as some children sing the phrase *puff, puff, puff*. Praise those children who do sing alone, and make a note of their tonal and rhythm development.

ASSIMILATION

After children and caregivers are familiar with the previous Imitation Activity, have them sway as they audiate the phrase, *Jeremiah, blow the fire*, and then sing and sway the phrase, *puff, puff, puff*. Each child and caregiver should demonstrate the scarf-blowing activity described in the Acculturation Activity at the end of each repetition. Use the following preparatory phrase to assist in audiating meter, tempo, tonality, and starting pitch.

Roll the Ball Like This

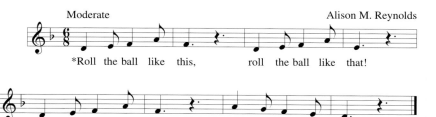

Moderate   Alison M. Reynolds

*Roll the ball like this, roll the ball like that!

Roll the ball like this, roll the ball like that!

*Change to "Bounce"

MUSIC CONTENT

Harmonic Minor Tonality

Usual Triple Meter

MOVEMENT CONTENT

FLOW
Continuous Flow

WEIGHT
Strong, Gentle

SPACE
Stationary

COORDINATED BREATHING
Audiating, Moving, Singing

MATERIALS NEEDED

Space for free movement

Tennis balls, one per child

ACCULTURATION

Sing *Roll the Ball Like This* while modeling continuous flow. Pause briefly between each repetition of the song. During the silences, model a deep breath while bringing both arms behind you and back. As you exhale, bring arms forward as though you are rolling a large ball. Pause again, and repeat the song. When you are rolling the imaginary ball, sometimes demonstrate strong rolling movements, and other times demonstrate gentle rolling movements.

IMITATION

(1) Pair each child with an adult or another child. Give each pair a tennis ball. Model taking a deep breath and then rolling the ball to your partner and have your partner take a deep breath and roll the ball back to you. Tell children that when they hear singing, the balls should be still, but when the singing stops, they are to breathe and roll the ball. (2) Find another adult to be your partner. Model breathing and preparing to roll the ball so you release as you begin the singing the song. Your partner will take the ball and repeat the movements. Model rolling the ball each time you hear the word *roll* in the song.

ASSIMILATION

(1) Repeat the Imitation Activity above, this time adding a new movement to replace rolling the ball. Instead, breathe and flick your hands each time the word *bounce* appears in the song. After children have coordinated their breathing and moving, model breathing and bouncing the ball while you sing. (2) Sing the song, but do not sing the last part: *Roll the ball like that!* Invite children to sing the part of the song that is missing. Give individual children an opportunity to sing the end of the song as they roll their ball to you.

My Pony Bill

Moderate

Angela Wiechard

My po - ny Bill is rid - ing high. See my po - ny

gal-lop-ing by. My po - ny Bill is rid - ing high. See him gal-lop-ing by.

MUSIC CONTENT

Harmonic Minor Tonality

Usual Triple Meter

MOVEMENT CONTENT

FLOW
Bound, Free

SPACE
Locomotor

MATERIALS NEEDED

Space for free movement

Stuffed animals

ACCULTURATION

Perform the song using the text. Take a favorite stuffed animal and dance it around the children as you sing.

IMITATION

Perform the song using the text as you gallop around the room. Encourage the children to gallop with you. Substitute each of the following words for the word *gallop* as variations: *trotting, swimming, walking.* Encourage them to perform each of the movements as a pony would. Some may choose to do this on all fours. Some may choose to do this while standing.

ASSIMILATION

Perform the song as in the previous Imitation Activity and add expressive qualities to each of the variations by having the children perform the movements in imaginary substances. For instance, have the children gallop in peanut butter, trot in glue, swim in feathers, and walk in ice cubes. Ask the children for their suggestions and perform them too.

Ni, Nah, Noh

Moderate   Wendy H. Valerio

Ni, nah, noh, ni, nah, noh, ni,——— nah, noh,—— ni,—nah noh.
Night- y night, night- y night, night - y night,—— night - y night.
I love you, I love you, I———— I—— I— love you.

MUSIC CONTENT

Aeolian Tonality

Usual Triple Meter

Ritard

Same and Different

MOVEMENT CONTENT

SPACE
Stationary

MATERIALS NEEDED

Space for free movement

ACCULTURATION

Sing the song using neutral syllables as the children are lying down or being rocked to take naps. You may also use this song to calm the children between performances of other activities. Sing the song and pretend to take a nap yourself. Encourage the children to pretend to take naps. The children will watch you or imitate you. Either response is a good response. Be sure to demonstrate the use of a deep inhalation between each phrase and repetition. Encourage the children to take deep breaths with you.

IMITATION

Perform the song as the previous Acculturation Activity. After several repetitions of the song, sing almost the whole song out loud, except the final note. Perform a slight *ritard* near the end of the song and then sing the final note in your audiation, but not out loud. Make eye contact with individual children as you do this.

ASSIMILATION

Perform the song as in the Acculturation Activity. After several repetitions of the song, tell the children that you will create a new ending to the song. You may use one of the examples provided below, or create your own. Ask the children if they can think of new endings to the song. Ask them to think of endings that are different from yours. Let those children who would like to perform those endings do so. Some children may sing exactly what you sang, some may not sing at all, and some may sing something different from you, yet the answer may not make much music sense. Some children may create an ending that is in tune and in meter.

1.   2.   3.   4.
I love you. I love you. I love you. I love you.

Bushes and Briars

Moderate   Traditional Britain

Through bush-es and through bri-ars—— I late-ly took my—
way.—— All—— for to—hear the new—— bird sing, and the
lambs to—skip and—play. All—— for to—hear the
new—— bird sing and the lambs to—skip and—play.

MUSIC CONTENT

Dorian Tonality

Usual Triple Meter

Same and Different

MOVEMENT CONTENT

FLOW
Continuous Flow

WEIGHT
Strong, Gentle

SPACE
Stationary

TIME
Quick, Slow

MATERIALS NEEDED

Space for free movement

ACCULTURATION

(1) Sing the song while modeling continuous flow. (2) Cradle a child in your arms, rocking her from side-to-side or front-to-back to the macrobeats while you sing. (3) Invite each child to stand behind a caregiver who is seated on the floor. Invite children to rock the caregiver front-to-back while you sing. Encourage caregivers to use a lot of space as they rock forward and back. If a child is doing the pushing movements, allow her to move in her own time.

IMITATION

(1) Model movements such as rocking, swinging, twisting, or bending to the macrobeats of the song. Invite children to perform the same movements. Observe children as they move. If children perform movements different from yours, include their movements as you model. (2) Tell the children this is a song about springtime, when baby birds and lambs are born. Ask them to perform light, quick movements of young birds or lambs. Then, ask them to pretend that there has been a terrific rainstorm after which the lambs have come out to play. Ask children to pretend that they are moving like lambs that are rolling in the mud left by the storm moving with strong and slow movements. Each time you present a new type of movement for the children, sing the song. Do not change the tempo of the song for quick or slow flowing movements.

ASSIMILATION

Tell the children that they are going to play as the birds and lambs do in the song. If you sing *Bushes and Briars,* they are to flow with slow, quick, strong, or gentle movements. If you sing another song, they are to freeze in self space. Begin singing *Bushes and Briars* and watch the children move. Then, sing another song and watch the children freeze their movements in self space. Repeat the process several times. Conclude the activity by leading the children in a discussion of their movements.

To the Window

Jane Kahan/Alison M Reynolds

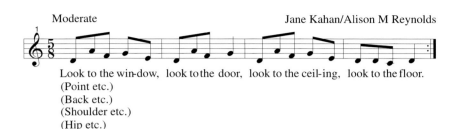

Moderate

Look to the win-dow, look to the door, look to the ceil-ing, look to the floor.
(Point etc.)
(Back etc.)
(Shoulder etc.)
(Hip etc.)

MUSIC CONTENT

Dorian Tonality or Aeolian Tonality

Unusual Paired

MOVEMENT CONTENT

BODY AWARENESS
Body Parts

FLOW
Continuous Flow

WEIGHT
Strong, Gentle

SPACE
High, Medium, Low Levels

TIME
Quick, Slow

COORDINATED BREATHING
Audiating, Moving, Chanting

MATERIALS NEEDED

Space for free movement

Long rope for everyone to
hold with two hands

ACCULTURATION

Sing *To the Window* moving your whole body with continuous flow. As you sing about specific body parts, emphasize that body part in your flowing movement. The song indicates different places in the room primarily to encourage your flowing movements to move about in space and to move at different levels (high, medium, and low). Between repetitions of the song, freeze during silences of varying lengths. Model differences in your flowing movements. Incorporate combinations of strong or gentle weight with quick or slow time.

IMITATION

Repeat the Acculturation Activity above, encouraging children to imitate your movements. If another child is moving and emphasizing flow with a body part different from yours, imitate her movements in the next repetition of the song, singing the name of the body part in the song that she was emphasizing.

ASSIMILATION

Move using continuous flow with pulsations to microbeats in the tempo children would expect you to perform *To the Window*. Invite children to audiate and to move as you are moving. When they begin to move, chant TAH to microbeats in Unusual Paired meter notated below. Ask children to chant TAH as they pulsate microbeats with flow. When they begin to chant, continue modeling continuous flow with pulsations, but do not chant TAH to microbeats. Instead, chant BAH to macrobeats notated below.

Microbeat Pattern

Tah   tah   tah   tah   tah

Macrobeat Pattern

Bah   bah

Swinging

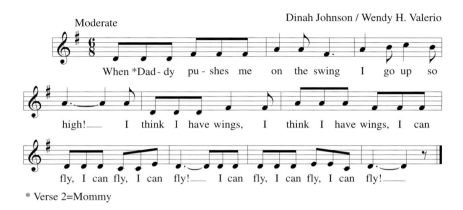

Moderate   Dinah Johnson / Wendy H. Valerio

When *Dad- dy pu - shes me on the swing I go up so

high!___ I think I have wings, I think I have wings, I can

fly, I can fly, I can fly!___ I can fly, I can fly, I can fly!___

* Verse 2=Mommy

MUSIC CONTENT
Mixolydian Tonality

Usual Triple Meter

MOVEMENT CONTENT
FLOW
Continuous Flow

WEIGHT
Strong, Gentle

SPACE
Stationary

TIME
Quick, Slow

MATERIALS NEEDED
Space for free movement

Elastic bands

ACCULTURATION

Distribute elastic bands, one to each caregiver. Show caregivers and children how to sit facing one another so that each can hold an end of the elastic band in both hands and row back and forth. Sing *Swinging* while you model rowing movements with another teacher or with another caregiver or child. If a child does not want to sit and row, invite those caregivers without a partner to model continuous flow in self space. As long as the children are safe and not distracting other children from hearing the music, the children are absorbing the music sounds as they play.

IMITATION

(1) Ask children to show you with their bodies the movement of a swing. Encourage them to demonstrate as many ways to swing their bodies that they can without talking. Then, ask them to perform one of the movements while you sing. If you are working with very young children who are imitating your movements, then simply model different types of swinging movements and encourage children to imitate those movements. (2) Invite caregivers to swing children as shown in the photograph on this page.

ASSIMILATION

Invite each child silently to decide whether to move their whole body with quick or slow continuous flow in self space while you sing *Swinging*. Remind them that in order for their whole bodies to move with continuous flow, they must include their hips, shoulders, and backs. Sing for the children and observe their movements. After you finish singing tell each child what you observed to discover if that movement was what the child intended. Repeat the activity asking them to choose strong or gentle flow. If necessary, model and label strong and gentle flow for the children. To encourage strong movements, ask them to pretend they are moving through peanut butter. To encourage gentle movements, ask them to pretend they are moving through bubbles they do not want to break.

Jerry Hall

Traditional, arr. Alison M. Reynolds

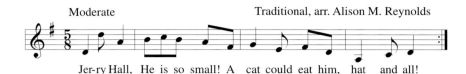

Moderate

Jer-ry Hall, He is so small! A cat could eat him, hat and all!

MUSIC CONTENT
Mixolydian Tonality

Unusual Paired

MOVEMENT CONTENT
FLOW
Continuous Flow

SPACE
Stationary

MATERIALS NEEDED
Space for free movement

One bean bag per person

One hula hoop per two people

ACCULTURATION

(1) Give each child and caregiver a bean bag. Place a bean bag on the back of your palm and invite everyone to do the same. Sing *Jerry Hall* while taking a bean bag for a continuous flowing ride. When you finish the song, freeze your movements and your voice. After a pause, resume singing and flowing, again freezing at the end of the song. (2) Repeat the move and freeze activity described in (1). This time, sing the resting tone pattern notated below when you freeze your movements. Then, stay frozen and silent before you resume singing. As you continue, sing the variation on the first pattern suggested when you freeze.

Variation

IMITATION

(1) Sing *Jerry Hall* and model rocking from side-to-side to macrobeats. Encourage everyone to imitate your movements. Be certain that you are still moving comfortably with relaxed flow between macrobeats. (2) Give a round hoop to each caregiver. Invite each child to stand opposite her. Both should hold on to the hoop with their palms facing down. The caregiver should stay kneeling on the floor so that she is roughly the same height as her child. Model rocking from side-to-side to macrobeats while you sing *Jerry Hall*.

ASSIMILATION

Place the hoops flat on the floor in a random pattern. Stand in the center of one of the hoops and model a jump out of the hoop. Invite children to practice jumping. Then, invite them to jump into the hoop. Finally, tell children that you will sing *Jerry Hall*. When you are singing, there should be no jumping, but when the song is over, they should jump from place-to-place and use as much space as possible. Encourage them to swing their arms, bend their knees, and breathe as they prepare and complete each jump.

The Wind

Moderate

Dinah Johnson/ Wendy H. Valerio

The wind is whist-ling through the trees, the wind is blow-ing

down the leaves and they fall, fall, fall,— and they fall, fall,

fall.— The wind is play-ing a friend-ly game, the wind is whis-per-

ing my name, as it calls, calls, calls,— as it calls, calls, calls.—

MUSIC CONTENT

Lydian Tonality

Usual Triple Meter

MOVEMENT CONTENT

BODY AWARENESS
Body Parts

FLOW
Continuous Flow

WEIGHT
Strong, Gentle

TIME
Quick, Slow

MATERIALS NEEDED

Space for free movement

ACCULTURATION

Make some whistling wind noises, and move as if you are a leaf being blowing around on a blustery day. Eventually fall gently to the floor and sing the song as you rock back and forth. Then sing each student's name using the following patterns. Take a big breath and move like a floating, flying leaf as you sing each child's name. Move differently for each child. Show extremes of quickness and extremes of slowness. Be sure to emphasize the movement of shoulders, backs, hips.

Ma - ri- a,   Kel- ly,   Ad-di-son, Ne - kein-dra   T. J.

IMITATION

Perform the song and movements as in the previous Acculturation Activity, however emphasize the movement of different body parts when you sing each child's name. Demonstrate a quick or slow movement for each of the following body parts, one body part for each child's name: head, neck, shoulder, back, arm, elbow, wrist, hip, knee, ankle, foot. Encourage the children to imitate your singing and moving.

ASSIMILATION

Perform the song and movements as in the previous Imitation Activity, however, allow individual children to sing and move their own names. Have the class copy the singing and moving of each child.

Poor Bengy

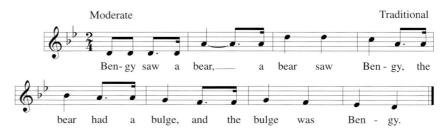

Moderate   Traditional

Ben-gy saw a bear,____ a bear saw Ben-gy, the

bear had a bulge, and the bulge was Ben - gy.

MUSIC CONTENT

Phrygian Tonality

Usual Duple Meter

MOVEMENT CONTENT

FLOW
Continuous Flow

SPACE
Stationary
Open Shapes
High, Medium, Low Levels

MATERIALS NEEDED

Space for free movement

ACCULTURATION

(1) Sing *Poor Bengy* for the children while moving with continuous flow using your whole body. Ask caregivers to move like you. Then, breathe and sing the resting tone and follow it with silence to create a brief pause. Repeat this activity several times. (2) Follow directions for Acculturation Activity (1). Then, breathe and sing the resting tone again and invite the caregivers to sing it after they take a breath. Ask them to audiate that sound (resting tone) silently, and to be ready to sing it at the end of the song. You will give them a breath gesture when you want them to sing it. Repeat the song, with all adults modeling continuous flow. At the end of the song, insert a silent pause. Then, give a breath gesture for the caregivers to breathe and sing the resting tone. (3) Set up a resting tone accompaniment to macrobeats for a second teacher or for all of the caregivers to perform. After an introduction of four macrobeats, sing *Poor Bengy* with the caregivers' accompaniment.

IMITATION

Invite children to stand and ask them to find and face a partner. The partner may be a caregiver or another child. While standing, invite the pairs to hold hands and begin performing a gentle swimming movement. When all or most of the pairs are moving with slow flow, begin singing *Poor Bengy* in unison. At the end of the song, sing one of the tonal patterns notated below. Take turns swimming with individual children. Sing each pattern and encourage each of your partners to repeat after you. Remind all adults to make eye contact and smile while gently swimming.

ASSIMILATION

(1) Model open shapes for children at high, medium, and low levels. Tell the children to make shapes just like yours. Label those shapes as open (Open shapes have empty space between body parts.). Breathe and sing combinations of patterns notated below for each open shape. (2) Repeat the activity, asking children to make an open shape that is not the same as yours.

North and South

Moderate   Dinah Johnson/ Wendy H. Valerio

I have just one   nose,   I have just one   mouth,   my

nose   is   north,   and my   mouth   is   south!

ACCULTURATION

Perform the song using text. Roll your hands in continuous motion and touch your nose on the word *nose*. Then, roll your hands in continuous motions and touch your mouth on the word *mouth*. Stretch continuous to the ceiling when singing, *My nose is north,* and stretch continuously to the floor when singing, *My mouth is south.* Expect the children to observe you, but do not expect them to copy your movements or singing.

IMITATION

Perform the song as in the previous Acculturation Activity; however, use a chiffon scarf as you move. Toss the scarf into the air when singing the words *nose* and *mouth.* Catch your scarf after each toss. Give each child and caregiver a chiffon scarf and encourage them to move, toss, and catch like you are.

ASSIMILATION

Perform the song as in the previous Imitation Activity; however, do not sing out loud on the words *nose* and *mouth.* Audiate and toss when you perform those words. You will perform each of those words twice. Encourage the children and caregivers to do the same.

MUSIC CONTENT

Locrian Tonality

Usual Duple Meter

MOVEMENT CONTENT

BODY AWARENESS
Body Parts

FLOW
Continuous Flow

MATERIALS NEEDED

Space for free movement

One chiffon scarf per person

chants
with
words

My Mother, Your Mother

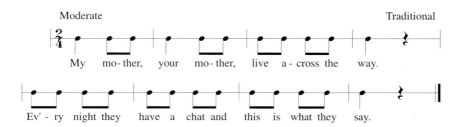

Moderate   Traditional

My mo-ther, your mo-ther, live a-cross the way.

Ev'-ry night they have a chat and this is what they say.

MUSIC CONTENT
Usual Duple Meter

MOVEMENT CONTENT
FLOW
Continuous Flow
Continuous Flow with Pulsations

MATERIALS NEEDED
Space for free movement

ACCULTURATION

Perform the chant using the text and improvise rhythm patterns between each repetition. If you are teaching alone, have a rhythm conversation with yourself, being certain to use an expressive voice as you chant. If you teaching with caregivers, have them copy your rhythm patterns, each four macrobeats in length. Use much expression in your conversations. Be dramatic. Let your body flow and assist with your animation. Do not expect the children to copy your rhythm patterns.

IMITATION

Perform the chant as in the previous Acculturation Activity; however, ask the caregivers to create their own rhythm patterns in answer to each of yours. Tell them to be different from you in their answers. Remind them to be dramatic and animated in their chants and their bodies. Expect the children to be chanting with you, and make note of those who are chanting patterns in answer to yours.

ASSIMILATION

Perform the chant as in the Acculturation Activity; however, have individual children copy your patterns. Then, perform the chant as in the Imitation Activity; however, have individual children create rhythm patterns that are different from yours.

Popcorn

MUSIC CONTENT
Usual Duple Meter

MOVEMENT CONTENT
FLOW
Continuous Flow
Continuous Flow with Pulsations
SPACE
Stationary, Locomotor
COORDINATED BREATHING
Audiating, Moving, Chanting

MATERIALS NEEDED
Space for free movement

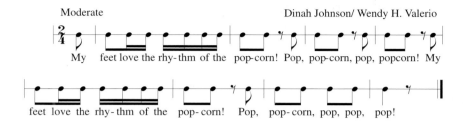

Moderate   Dinah Johnson/ Wendy H. Valerio

My feet love the rhy-thm of the pop-corn! Pop, pop-corn, pop, popcorn! My

feet love the rhy-thm of the pop-corn! Pop, pop-corn, pop, pop, pop!

ACCULTURATION

(1) With very young children and infants, ask adults to have children lie on their backs facing the adults. Ask adults to hold children's feet, and to gently swim them as they listen to you chant. Invite adults to join in chanting when they know the chant. Change the word *feet* in the chant to *hands,* and ask caregivers to continue the swimming movements with infants' hands. Repeat the activity. (2) With older children, model lying on your back with your feet up, and move your feet as though you are peddling a bicycle while chanting. Then, peddle your hands and feet in the air. Ask adults to move as you are moving and to chant with you.

IMITATION

(1) Invite caregivers to lie on their backs, pull their knees to their chests, and each put a child on his knees so they may bounce to the macrobeats during one repetition of the chant, and then to the microbeats during the next repetition of the chant. (2) Have caregivers model walking movements to the macrobeats during one repetition and then to microbeats during the next repetition. (3) After several repetitions of the chant, improvise 4, four-macrobeat patterns in Usual Duple meter on the syllable *Pop.* After you have finished, encourage children to make popcorn sounds like you have just made as you all continue walking. Let the children make their responses randomly. Do not expect their responses to be accurate in tempo or in meter. Then, invite individual children to chant Pop-ping patterns.

ASSIMILATION

Ask children to audiate and move with continuous flow, pulsating microbeats. Model the same movement, and then breathe and chant a four-macrobeat pattern on neutral syllables in Usual Duple meter. Show them a breath gesture and remind them what the gesture means. Then breathe, move, and chant a four-macrobeat pattern, giving the breath gesture on the fourth macrobeat of your pattern. The gesture ends with a flick indicating when the children should begin chanting. If children consistently coordinate their breathing with their movement and thier precise chanting, they are ready for rhythm pattern instruction appropriate for formal audiation instruction.

Go and Stop

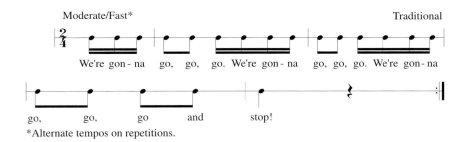

Moderate/Fast*   Traditional

We're gon-na go, go, go. We're gon-na go, go, go. We're gon-na

go,   go,   go   and   stop!

*Alternate tempos on repetitions.

MUSIC CONTENT

Usual Duple Meter

MOVEMENT CONTENT

FLOW
Continuous Flow
Continuous Flow with Pulsations

SPACE
Stationary, Locomotor

COORDINATED BREATHING
Audiating, Moving, Chanting

MATERIALS NEEDED

Space for free movement

ACCULTURATION

Perform the chant using netural syllables. Hold a child as you continuously move around the room, or let children watch you continuously move around the room. Emphasize the continuous movement of your shoulders, back, and hips as you travel. Freeze on the final macrobeat of the chant. Then, take a breath and move continuously as you perform *shhh*.... Repeat the process several times.

IMITATION

(1) Perform the chant using text. Move continuously around the room emphasizing your shoulders, back and hips. Freeze on the word stop. Then, take a breath and move continuously in place as you perform *shhh*..... Repeat the process several times. (2) Repeat with the following variations substitute for the word *go*: *swim, rock, wiggle, twist, sway, stretch.* (3) Perform out loud the anacrusis *We're gonna,* and then silently audiate and move the first, second, and third measures of the chant. Perform the words *and stop* out loud and freeze when you perform the word *stop*. Then, take a breath and move continuously in place as you perform *Shhh*.....Repeat with the following variations substitute for the audiated word *go*: *swim, rock, wiggle, twist, sway, stretch.*

ASSIMILATION

Perform the chant as in each of the Imitation Activities described above; however, emphasize continuous flow with microbeat pulsations. After the children are familiar with that activity, perform the chant and have the children perform continuous flow with microbeat pulsations as they chant TAH to each microbeat.

Sidewalk Talk

MUSIC CONTENT

Usual Duple Meter

MOVEMENT CONTENT

BODY AWARENESS

FLOW
Continuous Flow with Pulsations

SPACE
Locomotor
Directions

MATERIALS NEEDED

Space for free movement

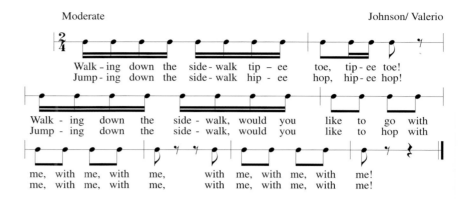

Moderate   Johnson/ Valerio

Walk - ing down the side - walk tip – ee   toe, tip - ee toe!
Jump - ing down the side - walk hip - ee   hop, hip - ee hop!

Walk - ing down the side - walk, would you   like to go with
Jump - ing down the side - walk, would you   like to hop with

me, with me, with me,   with me, with me, with me!
me, with me, with me,   with me, with me, with me!

ACCULTURATION

Perform the first verse of the chant using the text as you tiptoe to microbeats around the room. Make eye contact with children and encourage them to follow you, but to not expect them to tiptoe with an accurate steady beat. Encourage other caregivers to do the same. If necessary, carry a child with you as you go. Then, perform the second verse of the chant with the text. Jump from place to place when you chant the word *jumping*, and hop in place to macrobeats during the rest of the chant. Encourage the children to move like you are; however, do not expect them to do so with accuracy.

IMITATION

Perform the chant and movements as in the previous Acculturation Activity. Then, during verse 1 continue to tiptoe throughout the verse, and perform out loud only the following text: *Walking down the sidewalk,* and *With me, with me, with me.* Use eye contact to help you be dramatic as you audiate and move the rest of verse 1. During verse 2 continue to jump and hop as in the previous Acculturation Activity, but perform out loud only the following text: *Jumping down the sidewalk,* and *With me, with me, with me.* Use eye contact to help you be dramatic as you audiate and move the rest of verse 2.

ASSIMILATION

(1) Perform the chant and movements as in the previous Acculturation and Imitation Activities. Then, ask children for new ways to move down the sidewalk. They may suggest such movements as galloping, swimming, rolling, or turning. Incorporate each suggestion into a verse of the chant by moving in the way suggested by each child. Perform some variations of the chant with movement and full text out loud, and some with movement while silently audiating the chant. (2) Also try performing some variations while moving backward.

This Little Piggy

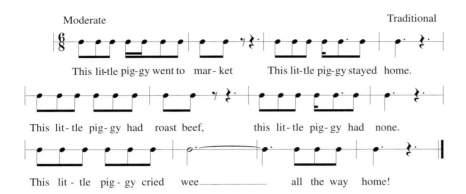

Moderate   Traditional

This lit-tle pig-gy went to mar-ket This lit-tle pig-gy stayed home.

This lit-tle pig-gy had roast beef, this lit-tle pig-gy had none.

This lit-tle pig-gy cried wee_____ all the way home!

MUSIC CONTENT

Usual Triple Meter

Ritard

Phrases

MOVEMENT CONTENT

BODY AWARENESS
Traditional actions corresponding to words

FLOW
Continuous Flow

SPACE
Stationary
Shapes

MATERIALS NEEDED

Space for free movement

Toes!

ACCULTURATION

Perform the traditional chant, wiggling one toe on a young child or toddler for each piggy in the rhyme. Begin with the big toe, and as you chant, *This little piggy cried*, gradually ritard the tempo of the rhyme. Resume the tempo when you say, *Wee! All the way home*. During this part of the rhyme, run your fingers up to the child's chin, and tickle him.

IMITATION

(1) Chant the rhyme, moving your whole body with continuous movement during the first phrase. During the second phrase, freeze. Continue alternating continuous movement with freezing for the rest of the rhyme. During the last phrase, continue moving with flow through the ritard. Encourage children to imitate your movements. (2) Establish a continuous flow conversation. Invite adults to be partners. During the first phrase, one adult models continuous flow in stationary space and freezes at the end. During the second phrase, the other adult moves with continuous flow in stationary space, freezing at the end of that phrase, and so on. During the last phrase, both you and the caregivers should move with continuous flow in locomotor space. Remind caregivers to try and use their whole bodies as they flow. Encourage children to imitate movements they see. Do not expect any particular movement from the children, and do not have them practice moving and freezing at precise times. Invite the children to do what you are doing.

ASSIMILATION

(1) Invite children to pick their favorite piggy from the rhyme, or ask each child to represent a different piggy through movement. When a child hears the part of the rhyme that represents his piggy, he should move his whole body with continuous flow making circular pathways with his hips, back, and shoulders. When he hears words that describe any other piggy, he should freeze in an open shape. (2) Repeat the activity, asking children to freeze in a closed shape.

Clackety Clack

MUSIC CONTENT

Usual Triple Meter

MOVEMENT CONTENT

BODY AWARENESS

FLOW
Continuous Flow
Continuous Flow with Pulsations

WEIGHT
Strong, Gentle

SPACE
Stationary

MATERIALS NEEDED

Space for free movement

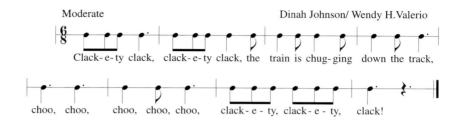

Moderate   Dinah Johnson/ Wendy H. Valerio

Clack-e-ty clack, clack-e-ty clack, the train is chug-ging down the track,

choo, choo, choo, choo, choo, clack-e-ty, clack-e-ty, clack!

ACCULTURATION

(1) Ask caregivers to place infants and toddlers on their laps facing them. Invite the caregivers to bounce children to macrobeats on their knees while you chant *Clackety-Clack.* Invite them to join in chanting after they have listened a few times. (2) Perform the chant several times through, each time inserting a pause of varying lengths between repetitions of the chant. Alternate strong bouncing movements as in Acculturation Activity (1) during one repetition, and holding hands and moving with gentle swimming movements during the next repetition. Encourage each caregiver to smile and make eye contact with his child as he moves.

IMITATION

Perform a macrobeat accompaniment on a full, strong *Chhh* train sound in the tempo children would expect you to perform. Invite adults in the room to perform your ostinato. Stand in self space and perform movements such as rock, push, pull, swing, and stretch in self space to the ostinato. Encourage children to imitate your movements as you chant *Clackety Clack* and the adults move and perform the ostinato.

ASSIMILATION

(1) Move your whole body with continuous flow and encourage children to do the same. Audiate *Clackety-Clack* in the tempo the children would expect you to perform. Add microbeat pulsations to your continuous flow, being certain to put pulsations in a different place each time. Ask children to add pulsations to their flow and to chant TAH to the microbeats in the tempo you are moving. (2) Assist children in establishing the pulsating with chanting. Tell them that when they hear *Clackety-Clack,* they are to continue pulsating, but to silently audiate TAH for each microbeat. When you stop *Clackety-Clack,* they are to resume chanting TAH while they pulsate microbeats.

Hickety Pickety Bumble Bee

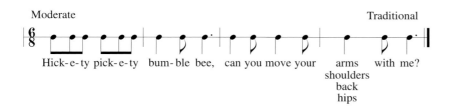

Moderate   Traditional

Hick-e-ty pick-e-ty bum-ble bee, can you move your arms with me?
shoulders
back
hips

MUSIC CONTENT

Usual Triple Meter

MOVEMENT CONTENT

BODY AWARENESS
Body Parts

FLOW
Continuous Flow
Continuous Flow with Pulsations

MATERIALS NEEDED

Space for free movement

ACCULTURATION

Chant *Hickety Pickety Bumble Bee* while moving with continuous flow. For each body part you insert in the chant, emphasize moving that body part with continuous flow using circular pathways. Remember to move as much of your body as you can, regardless of which body part is labeled in the chant. Invite caregivers to make eye contact and smile at children as they move and chant.

IMITATION

(1) Repeat the Acculturation Activity, this time encouraging children to imitate your movements. (2) At the end of the chant, perform 4 four-mac-robeat patterns in Usual Triple meter on a neutral syllable. Continue to move as you chant.

ASSIMILATION

(1) Model continuous flow and ask the children to move as you are moving. Audiate *Hickety Pickety Bumble Bee* silently in the tempo and meter the children would expect you to perform. Then, begin pulsating microbeats in the tempo you were audiating. (Be certain to pulsate the microbeats in different places in space so that you continue flowing.) Ask children to change their movements to pulsating movements like yours. When all or most of the children are moving, chant TAH to microbeats and ask children to do the same. As soon as they begin chanting and moving, you begin chanting BAH to macrobeats. (2) After children have completed the Assimilation Activity (1), ask children to continue pulsating and chanting TAH to microbeats while you chant *Hickety Pickety Bumble Bee* with text. Tell them that sometimes you will perform the chant out loud, and sometimes you will silently audiate the chant. Children are to continue audiating, pulsating, and chanting their part whether you chant aloud or silently audi-ate.

Here is the Beehive

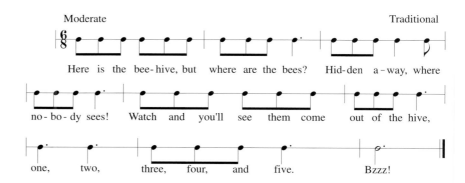

Moderate   Traditional

Here is the bee-hive, but   where are the bees?   Hid-den a-way, where

no - bo - dy sees!   Watch   and   you'll   see   them   come   out of the hive,

one,   two,   three,   four,   and   five.   Bzzz!

MUSIC CONTENT

Usual Triple Meter

Tempo: Quick, Slow

MOVEMENT CONTENT

BODY AWARENESS
Traditional finger-play actions

FLOW
Continuous Flow

WEIGHT
Strong, Gentle

SPACE
Locomotor
Pathways

TIME
Quick, Slow

COORDINATED BREATHING
Audiating, Moving, Chanting

MATERIALS NEEDED

Space for free movemen

ACCULTURATION

Perform the rhyme with corresponding hand actions.

1. *Here is the beehive,*
2. *But where are the bees?*
3. *Hidden away, where nobody sees.*
   Watch and you'll see them come out of the hive,
4. *1, 2, 3, 4, and 5!*
5. *Bzzzzzzz!!!!!!!!* (During the *Bzzz,* move your upper body and fingers with continuous flow and tickle a child. Repeat.)

IMITATION

(1) Perform the rhyme as in the Acculturation Activity above, this time modeling locomotor continuous flow using your whole body during the *Bzzz,* instead of tickling a child. Travel in random pathways using gentle, light, and quick movements. Encourage children to imitate your movements and your buzzing sound at the end of the rhyme. (2) Ask or remind children what bees are collecting when they come out of the hive (nectar). Invite them to listen to the rhyme again, and this time the chant will be about bees that have collected so much nectar, they can barely move. Perform the rhyme and gestures in a very slow tempo, using a voice that is also in slow motion. Augment the counting, and when you model continuous flow, move as slowly as possible. Encourage children to imitate your movements.

ASSIMILATION

Perform the rhyme for the children with the traditional finger-play. Invite the children to join you as they are comfortable with the gestures and the words. Model locomotor movements during the *Bzzz* as described in the first Imitation Activity. After you make the buzzing sound, do not stop moving with continuous flow. Instead, add pulsations to microbeats and chant TAH as you do so. Invite children to move with continuous pulsating flow to microbeats while they chant TAH. When they begin to chant TAH, you begin to chant BAH to macrobeats.

Jump over the Ocean

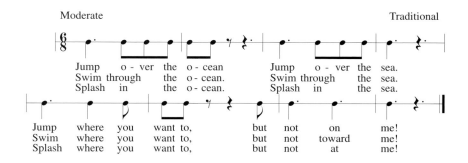

Moderate   Traditional

Jump   o - ver   the   o - cean   Jump   o - ver   the   sea.
Swim through   the   o - cean.   Swim through   the   sea.
Splash   in   the   o - cean.   Splash   in   the   sea.

Jump   where   you   want to,   but   not   on   me!
Swim   where   you   want to,   but   not   toward   me!
Splash   where   you   want to,   but   not   at   me!

MUSIC CONTENT

Usual Triple Meter

MOVEMENT CONTENT

FLOW
Continuous Flow

WEIGHT
Strong, Gentle

SPACE
Locomotor

MATERIALS NEEDED

Space for free movement

ACCULTURATION

Perform the chant using text. Allow each child to observe you as you perform jumps from one place to another each time you chant the word *jump*.
Be sure to swing your arms backward prior to each jump you perform to
assist in your demonstration of flow, weight, and proper breathing.

IMITATION

Perform the chant as in the Acculturation Activity. Encourage children to
jump as you do using a full arm swing. Substitute the following words for
the words *jump over*, and perform the indicated movements: *swim
through, splash in.* Perform several repetitions of each variation before
changing the words and movement.

ASSIMILATION

(1) Perform the chant several times as directed in the Imitation Activity.
Encourage the children to jump as you do. Then, ask the children to audiate
and move, but not to chant the word *jump* each time it appears in the
chant. Demonstrate and encourage the children to perform with you. (2)
Perform the new versions using the texts *swim through* and then *splash
in.* Instruct the children to audiate and move each of those phrases, but not
to chant them out loud. (3) Later, have the children also audiate and pat
the phrase *not on me* on their thighs. Offer a wink of encouragement
should any children or caregivers chant out loud as well as audiate and
move the indicated phrases.

Flop

Edwin E. Gordon

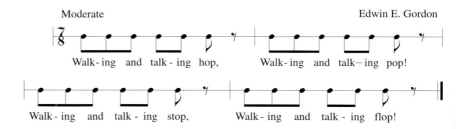

Moderate

Walk-ing and talk-ing hop,   Walk-ing and talk—ing pop!

Walk-ing and talk-ing stop,   Walk-ing and talk-ing flop!

MUSIC CONTENT

Unusual Unpaired Meter

MOVEMENT CONTENT

FLOW
Continuous Flow
Continuous Flow with Pulsations

SPACE
Locomotor

COORDINATED BREATHING
Audiating, Moving, Chanting

MATERIALS NEEDED

Space for free movement

ACCULTURATION

Perform the chant while modeling continuous flow with your whole body. Emphasize your hips, shoulders, torso, and back as you move those body parts in circular pathways. Resist the temptation to stop flowing at the end of each phrase of the rhyme. Encourage caregivers to model continuous flow and to chant with you as soon as they know the rhyme.

IMITATION

(1) Repeat the Acculturation Activity and encourage children to imitate your movements. Then, perform the rhyme without chanting out loud the rhyming words at the end of each phrase. Be certain to continue modeling continuous flow with your whole body and to maintain a steady tempo and meter as you chant. (2) Chant the rhyme again, this time standing in self space and moving as the words to the rhyme suggest. Perform walking movements to macrobeats.

ASSIMILATION

Audiate the rhyme in the tempo the children would expect you to perform it. Then, perform continuous pulsating flow to microbeats. Invite children to move the same way. Chant TAH to microbeats as in the pattern notated below, and invite children to join you. As soon as they begin chanting TAH to the microbeat pattern, chant BAH to macrobeats as in the second pattern notated below. Do not chant TAH with the children, as this is an opportunity for them to teach themselves how to coordinate their breathing with their movement and their breathing with their chanting.

Microbeat Pattern   Macrobeat Pattern

In the Tub

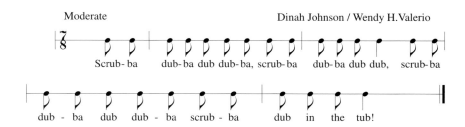

Moderate   Dinah Johnson / Wendy H. Valerio

Scrub-ba   dub-ba dub dub-ba, scrub-ba   dub-ba dub dub,   scrub-ba

dub - ba   dub   dub - ba   scrub - ba   dub   in   the   tub!

MUSIC CONTENT

Unusual Unpaired Meter

MOVEMENT CONTENT

BODY AWARENESS
Body Parts

FLOW
Continuous Flow

SPACE
Stationary, Locomotor

MATERIALS NEEDED

Space for free movement

One hula hoop per child

ACCULTURATION

Perform the chant using the text. Sit or stand and sway as you chant. Be creative with your swaying incorporating your shoulders, back, and hips with circular motions. Make eye contact with children and encourage them to move as you do.

IMITATION

(1) Stand and rock from side-to-side on macrobeats as you perform the chant using the text. Or, give each child a hula hoop, and tell them to sit inside the hoop, hold the hoop with both hands, and rock from side-to-side. Encourage children to rock like you, but do not expect them to rock accurately to macrobeats. (2) If there are other caregivers in the room, ask them to pretend to splash *ad libitum* with as many body parts as possible while you perform the chant. Encourage the caregivers to say *splash* each time they pretend to splash. You might suggest that they splash with elbows, backs, shoulders, hips, heels, or knees.

ASSIMILATION

(1) Stand and swing your arms from back to front on macrobeats as you perform the chant using the text. Encourage children to rock like you, but do not expect them to rock accurately to macrobeats. Draw attention to the proper placement of macrobeats by pretending to swim while splashing to the macrobeats of the following ostinato. Say *splash* each time you pretend to splash. Never splash in the same place twice in a row. Encourage the children to move and chant with you. (2) Later, try jumping each time you say *splash.* Be sure to swing your arms to help you jump. Encourage the children to move and chant with you.

Splash! Splash! Splash!

Hop and Stop

Edwin E. Gordon

MUSIC CONTENT

Multimetric: Unusual Paired, Usual Triple

MOVEMENT CONTENT

FLOW
Continuous Flow

SPACE
Stationary

MATERIALS NEEDED

Space for free movement

Beanbags

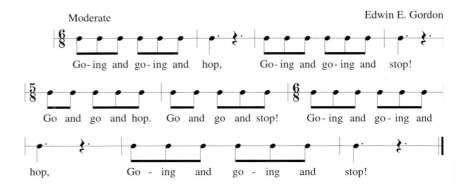

Moderate

Go- ing and go- ing and hop, Go- ing and go- ing and stop!

Go and go and hop. Go and go and stop! Go- ing and go- ing and

hop, Go - ing and go - ing and stop!

ACCULTURATION

Perform the chant with the text while standing. Move continuously and twist, sway, or swim when chanting all words except *stop* and *hop*. When chanting *stop*, freeze your movement; suspend your movement in time and space. When chanting *hop*, perform a hop in place. Allow the children to observe you as you move and chant.

IMITATION

Perform the chant as in the previous Acculturation Activity. Encourage children to move as you do, but do not expect them to move accurately. Vary the time and space each time after you chant and move the word *stop*. This will help children become aware of their own anticipation of the beginning of the chant.

ASSIMILATION

Give each child a beanbag. Tell the children to imitate your movement as you toss your beanbag and let it drop to the floor on the following words, *hop, pop,* and *stop*. Repeat the activity several times. Then, tell the children to audiate and move the chant, tossing their beanbags and letting them drop as if they were chanting the text out loud.

Glossary
Bibliography
and
Index

Glossary

Acculturation

The first type of preparatory audiation. It includes three stages. Typically children are in the first stage from birth to eighteen months of age, in the second stage from one to three years of age, and in the third stage from eighteen months to three years of age.

Arpeggioed Pattern

A tonal pattern in which almost all of the pitches move by skip, not by step. This type of pattern is performed for individual children in the Imitation and Assimilation types of preparatory audiation.

Assimilation

The third type of preparatory audiation. It includes two stages. Typically children engage in the Assimilation type of preparatory audiation from four years of age to five years of age. Some children may enter the first stage as early as three years of age and the second stage as early as four years of age.

Audiation

Hearing and formally comprehending in one's mind the sound of music that is no longer or may never have been physically present. It is different from discrimination, recognition, imitation, and memorization. There are eight types and six stages of audiation. Ideally, children begin to audiate when they are five years old, after they have phased through preparatory audiation.

Breath Gesture

A gesture that assists caregivers with performing a song, chant, tonal pattern, or rhythm pattern together as an ensemble, or with echoing a tonal or rhythm pattern in solo. For rhythm pattern guidance, the breath gesture should be given on the last macrobeat of the teacher's pattern. For tonal pattern guidance, slight pauses of varying lengths should occur after the teacher's pattern prior to the breath gesture.

Chant

In *Music Play,* music that is not perceived as being melodic and is not performed melodically.

Chord Root Accompaniment

Adding accompaniment by performing the root of the chords in harmonic rhythm as audiated or implied by the melody.

Classroom Activities

Music and movement activities other than tonal pattern or rhythm pattern guidance.

Continuous Flow

Free, flexible, smooth movement that is uninterrupted. Moving one's whole body with continuous flow requires moving the hips, back, shoulders in circular pathways and bending the knees.

Continuous Flow with Pulsations

Free and flexible movement that, while uninterrupted as in continuous flow, contains visual and physical representations of a consistent pulse. To insure that flow continues, each of the pulsations occurs in different a place in space. The pulsations are most effectively observed and felt when performed by a variety of body parts simultaneously.

Creativity	The spontaneous audiation and use of tonal patterns and rhythm patterns without restrictions.
Crescendo	A dynamic marking describing music that gradually becomes louder.
Decrescendo	A dynamic marking describing music that gradually becomes softer.
Developmental Music Aptitude	Music potential that is affected by the quality of environmental factors. A child is in the developmental music aptitude stage from birth to approximately nine years of age.
Diatonic Pattern	A tonal pattern in which the pitches move by half steps and whole steps but does not include chromatic pitches. This type of pattern is performed for individual children in the Acculturation type of preparatory audiation.
Division	A division of a microbeat or of a macrobeat (but is not a microbeat).
"Do" Signature	That which is traditionally called a key signature. It does not, however, indicate any one tonality or keyality. It does indicate where "do" is found on the staff.
Dominant Pattern	One function of tonal patterns. In major tonality it includes an arrangement of the tonal syllables "so ti re fa." In minor tonality it includes an arrangement of the tonal syllables "mi si ti re."
Dominant Pitch	The pitch of the fifth degree of the scale.
Dorian Tonality	The tonality of "re" to "re" with "re" as the resting tone. When compared to Harmonic Minor tonality, it has a raised sixth step and a lowered seventh step. The characteristic functions are tonic: all configurations of "re fa la," subtonic: all configurations of "do mi so," and subdominant: all configurations of "so ti re."
Duration	A part of a rhythm pattern. For example, each eighth-note in a rhythm pattern of two eighth-notes is a duration. A duration is to a rhythm pattern what a letter is to a word.
Echo	Repeat exactly what was previously just heard. Asking caregivers to be your echo is a useful way to invite them to participate in pattern guidance or in singing or chanting music during *Music Play* activities.
Eye Contact	In much the same way that young children respond to language when an adult speaks directly to them while looking directly at them, making eye contact with young children while performing music to them is an effective gesture that communicates to the children that they are important recipients of the adult's music.
Familiar Music	Music that has been returned to after performing different music.
Formal Instruction	Learning that is imposed upon children and promotes the development of their sense of objective tonality and objective meter. It usually takes place with children older than five, in terms of audiation, in a school. The emphasis is on cognition and learning what to audiate as well as how to audiate.

Harmonic Minor	The tonality of "la" to "la" with "la" as the resting tone. When compared to Major tonality, it has a lowered third and a lowered sixth step. The characteristic functions are tonic: all configurations of "la, do, mi," dominant: all configurations of "mi re ti si," and subdominant: all configurations of "la, re, fa."
Idiographic Evaluation	Evaluating a student by comparing that student's music achievement to his or her music aptitude or the student's current music achievement to his or her past music achievement.
Imitation	The second type of preparatory audiation. It includes two stages. Typically children engage in the Imitation type of preparatory audiation from three to four years of age. Some children may enter the first stage as early as two years of age and the second stage as early as three years of age.
Improvisation	The spontaneous audiation and use of tonal patterns and rhythm patterns with restrictions.
Informal Guidance	The basis of *Music Play,* a sequenced curriculum of Acculturation, Imitation, and Assimilation designed to encourage children who are in preparatory audiation to respond naturally and spontaneously to music. In informal guidance, children are not expected to respond to music. Children are simply exposed to music in the home or in a preschool. The emphasis is on intuition and learning how, not what, to audiate.
Keyality	The pitch name of the tonic. A keyality is audiated, whereas a key signature is seen in notation.
Level	A category of movement emphasizing space, describing how high or low in space the movement occurs in relation to another movement.
Locomotor Movement	Traveling from one place to another.
Locrian Tonality	The tonality of "ti" to "ti" with "ti" as the resting tone. When compared to Major tonality, it has a lowered second step, a raised fourth step, a lowered fifth step, and a raised eighth step. "So" is never used in Locrian tonality. The characteristic functions are tonic: all configurations of "ti re fa," subtonic: all configurations of "la do mi," mediant: all configurations of "re fa la."
Lydian Tonality	The tonality of "fa" to "fa" with "fa" as the resting tone. When compared to Major tonality, it has a raised fourth step. The characteristic functions are tonic: all configurations of "fa la do," dominant: (note this is not a seventh chord) all configurations of "do mi so," and supertonic: all configurations of "so ti re."
Macrobeat	The fundamental beat in a rhythm pattern.
Major Tonality	The tonality of "do" to "do" with "do " as the resting tone. When compared to Harmonic Minor tonality, it has a raised third step and a raised sixth step. The characteristic functions are tonic: all configurations of "do, mi so," dominant: all configurations of "so, fa, re, ti," and subdominant: all configurations of "fa, la, do."

Measure Signature	Traditionally called a time signature or a meter signature. A measure signature, however, indicates neither meter nor time. It indicates only the fractional value of a whole note that will be found in a measure. Because measure signatures are enrhythmic, a measure signature cannot indicate any one meter. Tempo markings and metronome markings indicate tempo, measure signatures do not.
Melodic Pattern	The combining of a tonal pattern and a rhythm pattern.
Melodic Rhythm	The rhythm of the text or the melody in a piece of music. It is superimposed on macrobeats and microbeats.
Memorization	Repeating without the use of notation music that was read or heard, but not necessarily audiated.
Meter	That which is determined by the length of macrobeats, how macrobeats are divided, and how macrobeats are grouped.
Microbeats	The equal divisions of a macrobeat.
Mixolydian Tonality	The tonality of "so" to "so" with "so" as the resting tone. When compared to Major tonality, it has a lowered seventh step. The characteristic functions are tonic: all configurations of "so ti re," subtonic: all configurations of "fa la do," and dominant (note this is not a seventh chord): all configurations of "do mi so."
Movable "do" Syllables	The tonal system in which the placement and position of "do" are dependent on keyality. For example, C is "do" in the keyality of C; D is "do" in the keyality of D; and so on. (The ascending chromatic syllables are "do, di, re, ri, mi, fa, fi, so, si, la, li, ti, and do." The descending chromatic syllables are "do, ti, te, la, le, so, se, fa, mi, me, re, ra, and do." In the immovable or fixed "do" system, regardless of keyality, C is always "do.") The tonal syllable system that is recommended for use in *Music Play* is movable "do" with a "la" based minor.
Music Achievement	Accomplishment in music.
Music Aptitude	Potential to achieve in music.
Music Aptitude Test	A test to measure potential for achieving in music.
Music Babble	The "musical" sounds a young child makes before developing an objective sense of tonality and an objective sense of meter. Music babble is to music as speech babble is to language. It typically occurs from Stage 1 to Stage 4 of preparatory audiation.
Music Learning Theory	Music Learning Theory is the analysis and synthesis of the sequential manner in which we learn when we learn music.
Neutral Syllable	A nonsense syllable, rather than tonal syllables or rhythm syllables, used to perform a tonal or rhythm pattern or a song or chant without words.

Normative Evaluation	Comparing a child's music aptitude or music achievement with the music aptitude or music achievement of other children.
Notational Audiation	The audiation of what is seen in music notation without the aid of physical sound.
Note	A symbol that is read or written in music notation and represents what is being audiated.
Objective Keyality	A keyality for which there is consensus.
Objective Meter	A meter for which there is consensus.
Objective Tempo	A tempo for which there is consensus.
Objective Tonality	A tonality for which there is consensus.
Phrygian Tonality	The tonality of "mi" to "mi" with "mi" as the resting tone. When compared to Harmonic Minor tonality, it has a lowered second and a lowered seventh step. The characteristic functions are tonic: all configurations of "mi so ti," subtonic: all configurations of "re fa la," and supertonic: all configurations of "fa la do."
Pianissimo	A dynamic marking describing music that is performed very softly.
Pitch	A part of a tonal pattern. A pitch is to a tonal pattern what a letter is to a word.
Pitch Names	The letter names associated with the sounds of pitches, not letter names associated with a line or space on the staff.
Preparatory Audiation	Hearing and comprehending music while in the "music babble" stage, typically from birth to five years of age, as a readiness for engaging in audiation. There are three types of preparatory audiation - Acculturation, Imitation, and Assimilation - and seven stages of preparatory audiation.
Range	The distance between the lowest and highest pitches in the song.
Repetition	In *Music Play,* reference to performing a chant or song multiple times before beginning a different song or chant. Repetition does not necessarily mean to perform the same song or chant again immediately following a performance of that song or chant. Inserting silent pauses of varying lengths between performances of the same song or chant is recommended. Repetition also refers to returning to a song or chant as a familiar activity within a class time or within a session.
Resting Tone Accompaniment	Adding harmonic accompaniment by performing the root of the tonic chord throughout the song.

Resting Tone Sometimes referred to as the "scale tone" or a " home tone." A tonal center or centers to which a piece of music gravitates. A tonality has a resting tone, whereas a keyality has a tonic.

Rhythm That which consists of three fundamental parts: macrobeats, microbeats, and melodic rhythm. In audiation, microbeats are superimposed on macrobeats, and melodic rhythm is superimposed on microbeats and macrobeats.

Rhythm Pattern Two or more durations in a given meter that are audiated sequentially and form a whole.

Rhythm Syllables Different names that are chanted for different durations in a rhythm pattern. The rhythm syllables that are suggested for use with *Music Play* are based on beat functions rather than on the time-value names of notes.

Ritard Abbreviation for *Ritardondo* meaning slowing the tempo gradually.

Self Space The place where one is when she is not touching anything or anybody.

Shape A category of movement emphasizing space, describing how much space is created by the position of a body: open, closed, straight, or curvy.

Singing Quality The type of voice quality preferrably modeled by adults when performing songs for young children. For children, a singing voice quality is usually achieved in their initial audiation and singing range–D above Middle C to the A above Middle C. When modeling in this range, female adults should sing in their head voices and male adults should sing in their falsetto voices or in the octave below.

Space One of the four elements of movement identified, labeled, and analyzed by Laban that describes the proximity of two objects, two people, or a person and an object to one another. In *Music Play,* moving with an understanding of space is a readiness for audiating the proximity of beats, which affects the physical and mental use of time in-between beats.

Stabilized Music Aptitude Music potential that is no longer affected by environmental factors. A child enters the stabilized music aptitude stage at approximately nine years old, and he remains there throughout life.

Stationary Space Remaining in one place while moving or being still.

Structured Informal Guidance Guidance that is based upon a child's natural responses and a specific plan. It occurs in Acculturation, Imitation, and Assimilation, specifically Stages 3 through 7 of preparatory audiation.

Subdominant Pattern One function of tonal patterns. In major tonality it includes an arrangement of the tonal syllables "fa la do." In harmonic minor tonality it includes an arrangement of the tonal syllables "re fa la."

Subito	A dynamic marking describing an abrupt change in dynamics. Either the music is suddenly very loud, or suddenly very soft.
Subjective Keyality	A keyality for which there is no consensus.
Subjective Meter	A meter for which there is no consensus.
Subjective Tempo	A tempo for which there is no consensus.
Subjective Tonality	A tonality for which there is no consensus.
Syntax	The orderly arrangement of pitches and durations which establishes the tonality and the meter of a piece of music. Music has syntax but not grammar.
Tempo	(1) The speed at which rhythm patterns are performed, and (2) the relative lengths of macrobeats within and among rhythm patterns.
Time	One of the four elements of movement identified, labeled, and analyzed by Laban that describes movement initially as being sustained (slow) or quick. Eventually, the coordination of movement in time to music is emphasized.
Time-Value Names	The arithmetic fraction names given to durations relative to a whole note seen in music notation.
Tonal Pattern	Two to five pitches which collectively have unique musical meaning in a given tonality and a given keyality.
Tonal Syllables	Different names that are sung for different pitches in a tonal pattern. The tonal syllables that are used in *Music Play* are based on the movable "do" system with a "la" based minor.
Tonality	That which is determined by the resting tone. If "do" is the resting tone, the tonality is Major, if "la" is the resting tone, the tonality is Harmonic Minor, and so on. A tonality is always in a keyality, but a keyality may not be in a tonality.
Tonic	The pitch name of a keyality. For example, C, D, or Eb. A keyality has a tonic, whereas a tonality has a resting tone.
Tonic Pattern	One function of tonal patterns. In Major tonality, for example, it includes an arrangement of the tonal syllables "do mi so." In Minor tonality it includes an arrangement of the tonal syllables "la do mi."
Transition Stages	Stages 4 and 6 of preparatory audiation. A transition occurs from informal guidance to formal instruction in public school or private instrumental lessons.
Unfamiliar Music	Music that is heard for the first time. Although it is not clear how many repetitions makes music familiar, in *Music Play,* unfamiliar music includes the first series of repetitions of a new piece of music.

Unstructured Informal Guidance	Guidance that is based upon a child's natural responses and not on a specific plan. It occurs in Acculturation, specifically in Stages 1 and 2 of preparatory audiation.
Unusual Meter	Two types of meter in which macrobeats are of unequal length, regardless of whether they are audiated in pairs or more than a pair, whether some of them are intact, or whether they are divided into two or three microbeats.
Unusual Paired Meter	The meter that results when macrobeats of unequal length are audiated in pairs. Some macrobeats are divided into two and others into three microbeats of equal length.
Unusual Unpaired Meter	The meter that results when macrobeats of unequal length are audiated in more than a pair. Some macrobeats are divided into two microbeats others into three microbeats of equal length.
Upbeat	An anacrusis. The preparation for performing a macrobeat.
Usual Combined Meter	The meter that results when macrobeats of equal length are audiated in pairs. Some macrobeats are divided into two and others into three microbeats of unequal length.
Usual Duple Meter	The meter that results when macrobeats are of equal length and are audiated in pairs. Each macrobeat is divided into three microbeats of equal length.
Usual Meter	Three types of meter in which macrobeats are of equal length and are audiated in pairs. The macrobeats are divided into two and/or three microbeats, depending upon the meter.
Usual Triple Meter	The meter that results when macrobeats of equal length are audiated in pairs. Each macrobeat is divided into three microbeats of equal length.
Weight	One of the four elements of movement identified, labeled, and analyzed by Laban that describes the force behind a movement, such as strong or gentle.

Bibliography

Blesedell, D. S. (1991). A study of the effects of two types of movement instruction on the rhythm achievement and developmental rhythm aptitude of preschool children. *Dissertation Abstracts International,* 52 (07), 2452. (University Microfilms No. AAC9134919)

Chang, H. & Trehub, S. E. (1977). Auditory processing of relational information by young infants. *Journal of Experimental Child Psychology,* 24 (2), 324-331.

Gordon, E. E. (1997). *A music learning theory for newborn and young children.* Chicago: G.I.A.

Gordon, E. E. (1989). *Audie: A game for understanding and analyzing your child's music potential.* Chicago: G.I.A.

Gordon, E. E., Bolton, B. M., Hicks, W. V., & Taggart, C. C. (1993). *Experimental Songs and Chants, Book One.* Chicago: G.I.A.

Graziano, A. B., Shaw, G. L., & Wright, E. L. (1997). Music training enhances spatial-temporal reasoning in young children. *Early Childhood Connections,* 3 (3), 30-36.

Hicks, W. K. (1993). An investigation of the initial stages of preparatory audiation. *Dissertation Abstracts International,* 54 (04), 1277. (University Microfilms No. AAC9316493), Temple University, 1993.

Jacques-Dalcroze, E. (1921). Eurythmics, music, and education, trans. Harold F. Rubenstein. London: G. P. Putnam's Sons.

Jordon, J. M. (1996). *Evoking sound: fundamentals of choral conducting and rehearsing.* Chicago: G.I.A.

Jusczyk, P. W., & Krumhansl, C. L. (1993). Pitch and rhythmic patterns affecting infants' sensitivity to musical phrase structure. *Journal of Experimental Psychology, Human Perception and Performance,* 19 (3), 627-640.

Krumhansl, C. L., & Jusczyk, P. W. (1990). Infants' perception of phrase structure. *Psychological Science,* 1 (1), 70-73.

Laban, R. (1971). *The mastery of movement.* London: London MacDonald and Evans.

Littleton, D. (1989). Child's play: Pathways to music learning. in B. Andress (Ed.), *Prekindergarten music education* (pp. ix-xii). Reston, VA: Music Educators National Conference.

Metz, E. (1989). Movement as a musical response among preschool children. *Journal of Research in Music Education,* 37 (1), 48-60.

Moog, H. (1976). *The musical experience of the pre-school child,* trans. Claudia Clarke. London: Schott and Co.

Moorhead, G. E. & Pond, D. *Music of young children.* Santa Barbara, California: Pillsbury Foundation for Advancement of Music Education, 1977.

Music Educators National Conference (MENC) Task Force for National Standards in the Arts (1994). *The school music program: A new vision - The K-12 national standards, pre-K standards and what they mean to music educators.* Reston, VA: Music Educators National Conference.

Pond, D. (1992). The young child's playful world of sound. In B. Andress & L. M. Walker (Eds.) *Readings in early childhood music education* (39-42). Reston, VA: Music Educators National Conference.

Rauscher, F. H., Shaw, G. L., Levine, L. J., Wright, E., Dennis, W., & Newcomb, R. (1997). Music training causes long-term enhancement of preschool children's spatial-temporal reasoning. *Neurological Research,* 19, 2-8.

Reynolds, A. M. (1995). An investigation of the movement responses performed by children 18 months to 3 years of age and their caregivers to rhythm chants in duple and triple meters. *Dissertation Abstracts International,* 56 (04), 1283. (University Microfilms No. AAC9527531)

Sims, W. L. (1985). Young children's creative movement to music: categories of movement, rhythmic characteristics, and reactions to changes. *Contributions to Music Education,* 12, 42-50.

Trehub, S. E. (1987). Infants' perception of musical patterns. Special issue: The understanding of melody and rhythm. *Perception and Psychophysics,* 1987, 41 (6), 635-641.

Trehub, S. E., Thorpe, L. A., Trainer, L. A. (1990). Infants' perception of good and bad melodies. *Psychomusicology,* 9(1), 5-19.

Vaughn, C. (1996). *How life begins: the science of life in the womb.* New York: Times Books.

Weikart, P. S. (1982). *Teaching Music and Dance.* Ypsilanti: High/Scope Press.

Wilkin, P. E. (1995/1996, Winter). A comparison of fetal and newborn responses to music and sound stimuli with and without daily exposure to a specific piece of music. *Bulletin of the Council for Research in Music Education,* 127, 163-169.

Woodward, S. C. (1992). *The transmission of music into the human uterus and the response to music of the human fetus and neonate.* Unpublished doctoral dissertation, University of Cape Town, South Africa.

Index

About the Authors

Dr. Alison M. Reynolds is currently director of the Children's Music and Movement Development Program at Ashland University in Ashland, Ohio. She teaches music in the laboratory preschools on campus and has recently begun working with the Ashland County Preschool. Her work with children younger than five years of age began in 1988 when she began graduate studies in music learning theory and early childhood music with Dr. Edwin Gordon at Temple University. Dr. Reynolds is an early childhood music faculty member of the Gordon Institute for Music Learning certification program, and is a frequent presenter of workshops on the topics of early childhood and elementary general music.

Dr. Wendy H. Valerio is the founder and director of the Children's Music Development Center at the University of South Carolina, Columbia, where she teaches graduate and undergraduate courses in early childhood, elementary, and middle school music methods and music learning theory. After completing a B.M.E. at Baker University, Baldwin City, Kansas, Dr. Valerio taught elementary music education (K–6) in the public school system of Lawrence, Kansas and completed M.M. and Ph.D. degrees at Temple University in Philadelphia where she was coordinator of the Children's Music Development Program. Currently, Dr. Valerio, her graduate students, and undergraduate assistants co-teach weekly classes for young children (birth through grade 6) at the Children's Music Development Center, The Children's Place at South Carolina Educational Television, St. Peter's Catholic School, and the Center for Inquiry, all of Columbia, South Carolina.

Dr. Beth M. Bolton, assistant professor of music education at Temple University, is director of the Early Childhood Music Foundations program for children birth to five years old, an integral component of the Temple Music Preparatory Division. She teaches infants and toddlers in that program and coordinates a team of ten teachers. She has presented early childhood workshops and pedagogy sessions for the MENC and MTNA national conferences, for the Early Childhood Music Association, for several universities and state music educators associations. Dr. Bolton's early childhood research is focused on identifying musical behaviors in infants and toddlers.

Dr. Cynthia Crump Taggart received her B.M. and M.M. in Music Education from the University of Michigan and her Ph.D. in Music Education from Temple University. Currently, she is an Associate Professor of Music Education and Associate Director of Graduate Studies for the School of Music at Michigan State University. She also directs and teaches in the Early Childhood Music Program and Young Musicians Program of the Community Music School of Michigan State University's School of Music.

Edwin E. Gordon is known throughout the world as a preeminent research, teacher, author, editor, and lecturer in the field of music education. His pioneering 1989 book, A Music Learning Theory for Newborn and Young Children, was the first scholarly look at the critical importance of preschool music education.

Since 1997, Dr. Gordon has been Distinguished Professor in Residence at the University of South Carolina, following his retirement as the Carl E. Seashore Professor of Research in Music Education at Temple University in Philadelphia.

In addition to advising Ph.D. candidates in music education, Professor Gordon devoted many years to teaching music to preschool-aged children. Through extensive research, he has also made major contributions to the study of music aptitudes, stages and types of audiation, music learning theory, and rhythm and movement in music, to name just a few areas.

Before devoting his life to music education, Dr. Gordon earned degrees in string bass performance and played string bass with the Gene Krupa band.

Professor Gordon and his work have been portrayed nationally and internationally on the NBC Today Show, in the New York Times, in USA Today, and in a variety of European and Asian publications. He lives with his wife Carol in Columbia, South Carolina.